W9-AFC-380

make me I'm yours...

Jewellery

D&C
David and Charles
www.rucraft.co.uk

contents

Techniques

introduction

This book has all the inspiration and know-how you need to make your very own unique pieces. Never again will you have the embarrassment of arriving at the party to find someone wearing the same necklace as you, but when she see yours, she'll wish she was!

There are over 20 stunning designs to choose from, including lovely necklaces and beautiful bracelets, ravishing rings and amazing earrings. From vintage-inspirations to vibrant creations, there are styles to suit your mood today and tomorrow. Also you will be inspired to make your very own beads – which are so simple to create from easy to source materials such as fabric and polymer clay – and to discover some unusual jewellery-making techniques such as knotting. Each project has been rated to give you an idea of just how easy it is to make.

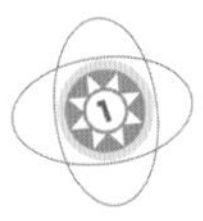

These are the simplest of projects to get you started on discovering the fun of making your own jewellery.

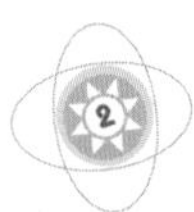

These projects are for when you are ready to explore a little and they give you so many more design options for your pieces.

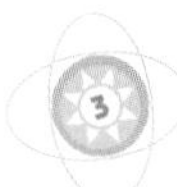

With some experience behind you, these projects will give you new challenges with some exciting wirework and beading techniques.

There are lots of ideas throughout for coordinating pieces or adapting the designs, so you'll never be short of inspiration. Next time a friend comes up to you and says: 'That's lovely – where did you get it?', be sure you can proudly say, 'I made it myself!'

vintage

2

ivory rose cuff

This wonderful cuff-style bracelet is a great way to start your adventure with wire and beads. Choose a bracelet blank that has loops through which you can thread beaded embellishments; ours is handmade copper with three loops to give plenty of room for the bright turquoise nuggets, luminous glass leaves, handmade ivory bead stacks, and beautiful vintage-style rose. We hope you have fun making your bracelet as unique as you are.

you will need

- one cream 2.5cm (1in) tea rose
- strand of turquoise 8–10mm side-drilled nuggets
- two vintage carved-ivory 7–8mm round beads
- forty vintage bone or ivory 4–5mm rondelles
- approx ten 1.5cm (⅝in) Bohemian glass leaves
- beige pearlized glass seed beads
- copper cuff with three loops, 5cm (2in) wide
- 0.6mm (24swg/22awg) copper wire
- side cutters
- round-nose pliers
- flat-nose pliers
- drill

1. Drill through the back of the flower (side-to-side) so that you can easily run wire through it. Cut an 18cm (7in) length of copper wire and run it through the flower. Centre the flower on the wire. Insert the ends of the wire through two of the loops on the bracelet. Wrap one end of the wire around the loop closest to the flower.

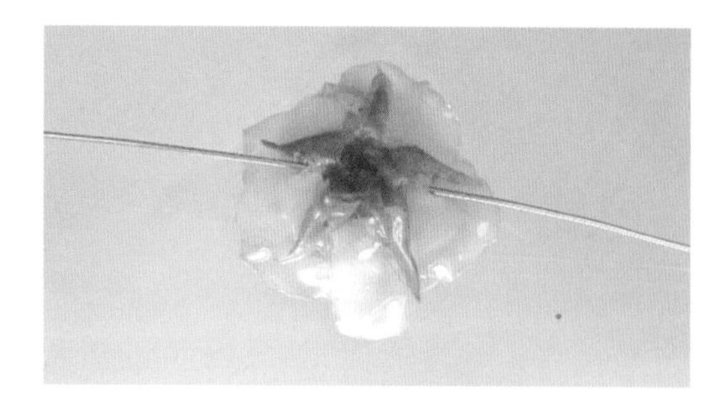

2. Add several turquoise nuggets. Wrap the wire around the flower again to tighten. Use round-nose pliers to coil the remaining end of the wire down to the base of the flower where it will not be seen when the bracelet is finished. Now start to build up the design around the flower. Always allow at least 18cm (7in) of wire when you are attaching the embellishments. Run the wire through a loop on the cuff or through the wires of beads that have already been secured to the bracelet.

3. To prepare the leaves before attaching, wrap the tail of the wire through the hole leaving about 2.5cm (1in) sticking out the other side. Twist the tail around the wire a couple of times before trimming the end with side cutters.

As you continue to add beads, keep as much of the wire hidden as possible, working it down under the beads to avoid a mass of wire showing on your finished design.

4. To prepare larger beads before attaching, run wire through the beads and make a tight coil at one end for decorative interest. Using round-nose pliers make a small 'U' shape on the end of the wire rather than a loop. Hold the 'U' sideways in flat-nose pliers and bend the straight wire around. Move the tiny coil around a few millimetres (⅛in). Bend the wire round against the loop. Keep rotating the coil and bending the wire around until it is the size required.

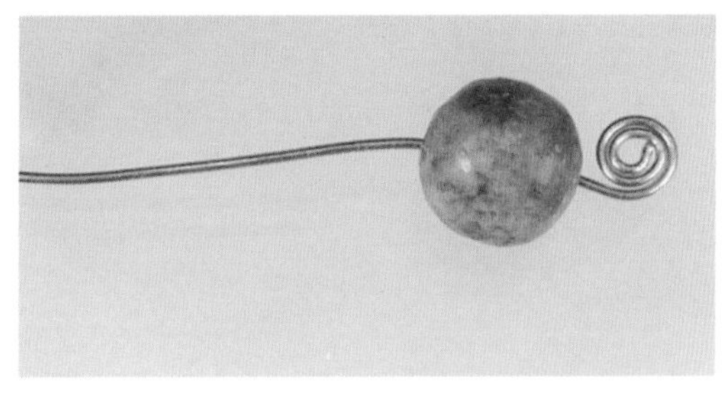

5. For the beaded stamens, add pearlized seed beads, rondelles and carved-ivory beads in combination. Tightly coil about 2cm (¾in) of wire against the bead stack at one end.

techniques ... string, wire & chain ... essential tools ... wirework techniques

1

classic bronze chain

This fabulous sautoir – French for 'long-chain necklace' – is a great way to make use of that collection of broken chains tangled together at the bottom of your jewellery box. Don't be afraid to make it long – they usually hang down as far as the tummy – and choose a large focal bead like ours to draw attention to the cute chain tassel. Why not make a couple more tassels to make yourself a stunning pair of matching earrings?

you will need

- six 15–20mm bronze metal round and oval beads
- four 25mm bronze metal square flat beads
- five 15mm cream glazed ceramic beads
- one 25 x 35mm brown cut-glass crystal
- three different styles of antique gold or bronze chains in mixed sizes, 30cm (12in) of each
- sixteen antique gold eyepins
- wire cutters
- round-nose pliers
- two pairs of flat-nose pliers

Look for unusual large beads or charms to create a focal point at the bottom of the necklace.

1. Make each bead into a bead link. Thread the bead onto an eyepin, bend the end of the eyepin over at an angle and trim to 7mm (⅜in). Use round-nose pliers to form the tail into a loop (see Techniques: Making a plain loop).

2. To make the tassel, join the large crystal to a ceramic bead. Attach six short lengths of chain to the loop below the ceramic bead.

3. Join each of the square beads to two other beads to make three groups of beads.

4. Cut short lengths of chain, between 5cm (2in) and 10cm (4in), and join two different styles to the wire loop above the crystal. Add a single bead link to one side and a group to the other.

5. Join the other bead links with chain in between, adding a plain length of chain to join the two ends that will sit at the back of the wearer's neck.

techniques ... essential tools ... making bead links and dangles

2

bird's nest earrings

Who would believe that these sweet 'enamel' earrings are actually made from a cardboard base? Vintage-style bird-and-nest stamped images have been accented with soft shades of blue and green ink coated with glaze, and the shiny surface is perfectly complemented by the coordinating crystal dangles. Just so long as you don't wear these earrings in the swimming pool, no one will ever know your secret!

you will need

- six 4mm green crystal rounds
- four 4mm jet black crystal rounds
- four 4mm light blue crystal bicones
- six 4mm gunmetal jump rings
- fourteen gunmetal headpins
- two earring wires
- two chipboard circles
- bird-and-nest stamp set
- inkpads: blue, green and black
- diamond glaze
- fine-tip black permanent marker
- round-nose pliers
- two pairs flat-nose pliers
- wire cutters
- hole punch

1. Punch a hole in each chipboard circle. Sponge green, then blue ink onto the front and back of each of the circles.

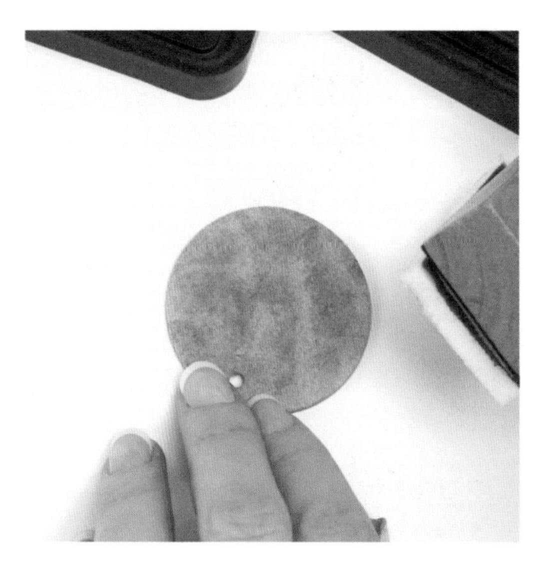

2. Once the ink has dried, stamp your chosen images onto each of the circles. Leave the ink to dry once again.

If you want to layer inks, let them dry between each application so the paper won't warp.

3. Apply a layer of diamond glaze to the front of the circles, taking care not to shake the tube to prevent bubbles. Allow the protective coating to dry before repeating on the back of the circles.

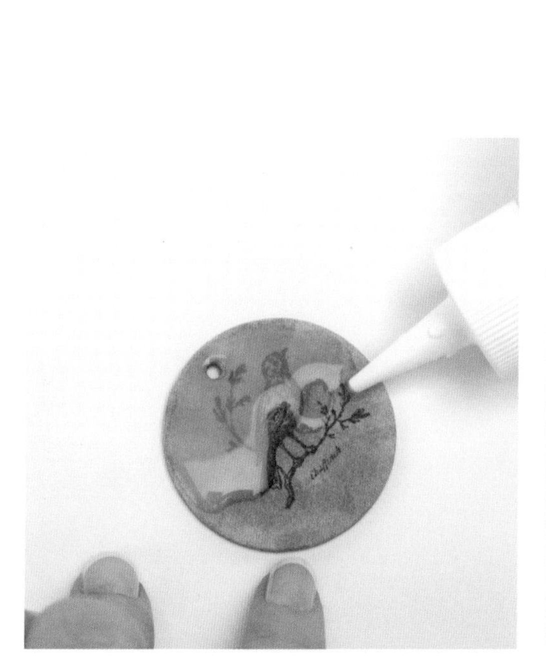

4. Lightly drag a fine-tip permanent marker around the edges of each circle to colour. Working from the back of the circle, insert the tip of the marker into the punched hole to accent.

5. Thread a 4mm green crystal round onto a headpin and thread the beaded headpin into the hole in the front of the decorated circle. Bend the headpin flush to the back of the bead and create a loop.

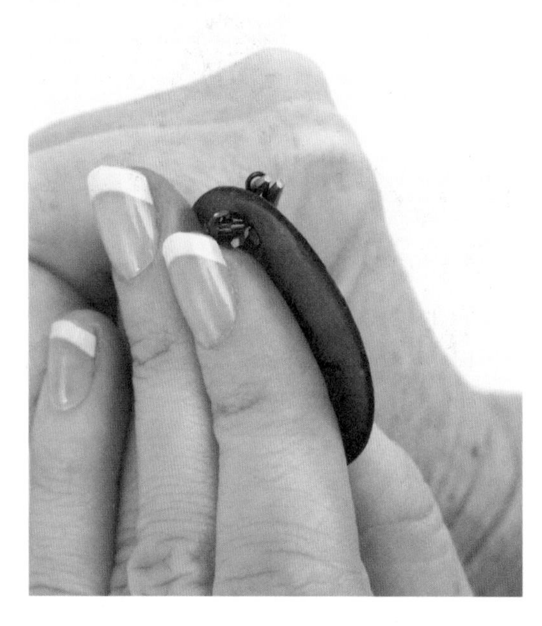

6. Slide each bead onto a headpin and make a wrapped loop above each bead (see Techniques: Making a wrapped loop). You will need six wrapped loop dangles (two of each bead colour) for each earring. Slide all of the dangles onto a jump ring and close. Secure the beaded jump ring onto the bail at the top of the embellished circle using a second jump ring. Use a third jump ring to secure to the earring wire.

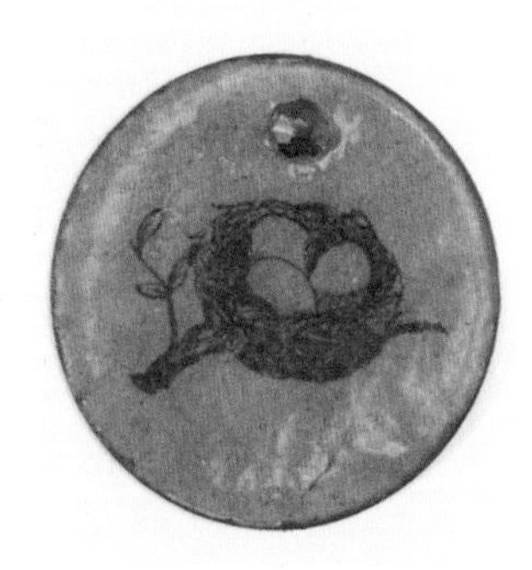

techniques ... making a wrapped loop ... opening and closing a jump ring

sweet little bird pin

A pre-cut chipboard bird and branch has been used to make this brooch. The check-effect on the bird was achieved by applying ink straight from the pads, and the branch was textured with various shades of brown and tan ink.

beaded leaf bracelet

When your jewellery making requires you to use materials such as 'memory' wire and 'miracle' beads, you know the results are going to be special, and this lovely little bracelet does not disappoint. The centre of our pretty cuff bracelet displays a vibrant mix of beads in an explosion of colours, while the wire tension makes the bracelet adjustable and holds it firmly in place around the wrist.

you will need

- bracelet memory wire
- two three-hole spacers
- turquoise Japanese seed beads
- selection of glass beads and size 6 and size 11 seed beads in turquoise, orange, peridot, brown and green
- turquoise miracle beads, various sizes
- round-nose pliers
- chain-nose pliers
- wire cutters

Miracle beads are so called because they look as if there is a bead inside the bead. To achieve this, the inside bead is sprayed repeatedly with a reflective material, then given a clear outside coating.

1. Allow the memory wire to coil around your wrist once and cut a piece to fit. Cut two more pieces to the same length. Shape a loop at one end of each of the pieces of wire using round-nose pliers. Squeeze the loop flat with chain-nose pliers.

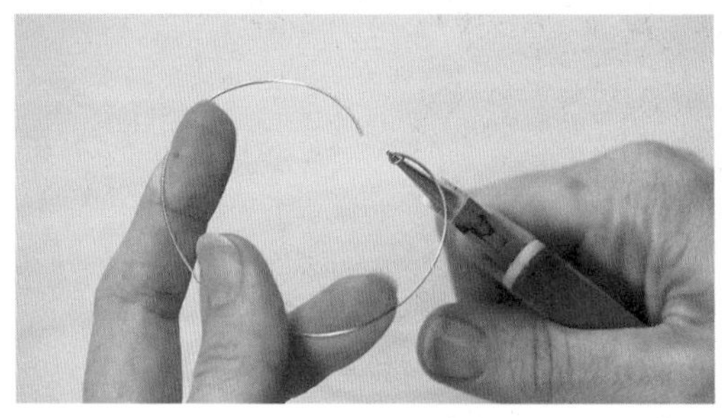

2. Take one piece of the memory wire and thread on one size 11 seed bead followed by fifteen Japanese seed beads. Add one size 6 seed bead, and thread the wire through the first hole in a three-hole spacer.

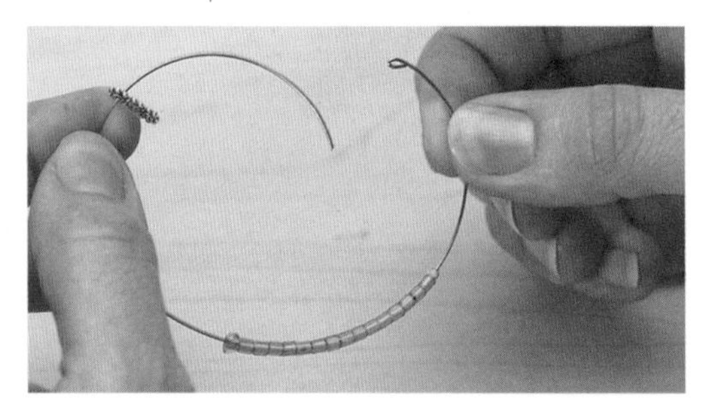

3. String about one half of the total length of the memory wire with a selection of colourful glass beads, including one or more turquoise miracle beads. Slide the wire through the first hole in a second three-hole spacer.

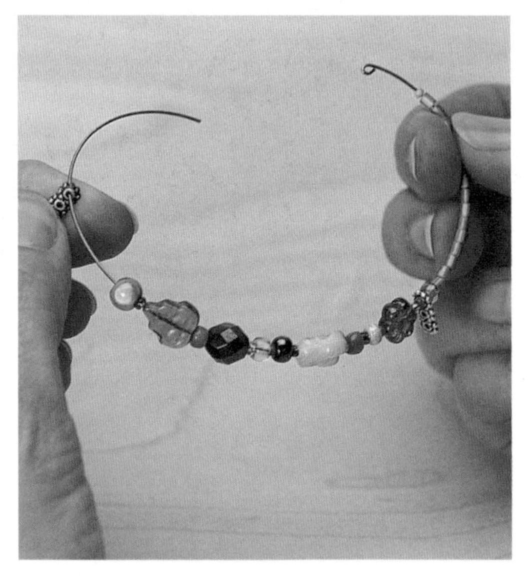

4. Continue adding beads to the end of the memory wire, stringing the pattern in step 2 in reverse. Fold over the end of the memory wire into a loop.

5. Taking a second piece of memory wire, repeat step 2, this time sliding the wire through the second (or middle) hole in the first spacer on the beaded piece of memory wire. Repeat steps 3 and 4.

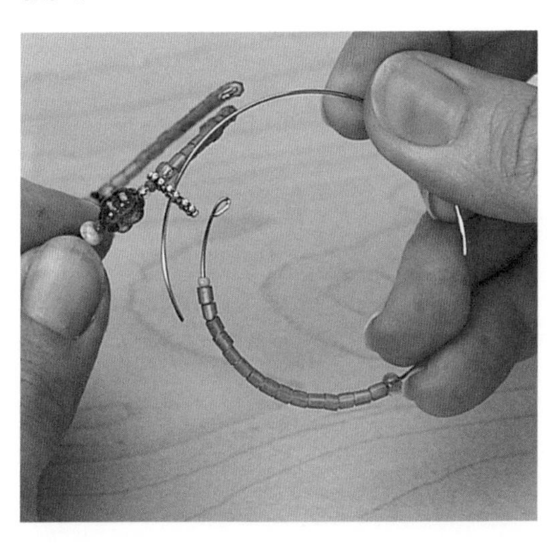

6. Taking the third piece of memory wire, repeat step 2, this time sliding the wire through the third hole in the first spacer on the beaded piece of memory wire. Repeat steps 3 and 4 to finish.

3

dazzling star ring

If your life is a little dull just now, get ready to bling it up with a fantastic piece of 'get yourself noticed' jewellery. This incredibly sparkly ring is made by working a rim of tiny seed beads, known as a bezel, over a large foil-backed stone or cabochon. Rounds of circular peyote stitch make a collar to keep the stone firmly in place, and a decorative twist is added to produce the spectacular star effect.

you will need

- one 12mm square aquamarine cabochon
- size 11 sea-green triangle beads
- size 15 turquoise galvanized cylinder beads
- size 15 silver charlottes
- size 15 crystal AB charlottes
- ring base
- size D bead stitching thread
- beading needle
- epoxy resin glue

Galvanized beads are electroplated with zinc for a metallic finish, while AB (meaning aurora borealis) beads have been treated with metal salts while the glass is hot for an iridescent, rainbow surface effect.

Condition the thread with wax before you begin to prevent the thread from slipping back through the bead after each stitch.

1. Pick up twenty triangle beads on a 1.5m (1½yd) length of thread, tie in a circle leaving a 15cm (6in) tail and then pass the needle through a few beads ready to work circular peyote stitch (see Techniques: Making a plain bezel). Pick up a triangle bead, miss a bead and pass through the next bead along. Continue all the way round, remembering to step up through two beads at the end of the round.

2. Add another round of triangle beads. Work a round of silver charlottes, a round of turquoise cylinder beads and finally a round of crystal AB charlottes. Pull the thread taut as you work and then take the needle through the beads to come out at the other side of the bezel between two triangle beads.

3. Insert the square stone face down in the bezel and repeat step 2 to secure the stone inside. Secure the thread with a half-hitch knot, then take the needle through the beads to come out in the centre row of triangles at the edge of the bezel.

4. To begin the herringbone stitch, pick up two cylinder beads, miss the next pair of triangle beads and pass the needle through the next triangle bead along. Pull the thread taut so that the cylinder beads are sitting almost side by side in a 'V' shape. Repeat all the way round. Step up through the first cylinder bead again ready to begin the next round.

5. *Pick up two cylinder beads and go down through the second cylinder bead added in the previous round. Pick up a silver charlotte and go up through the next cylinder bead along. Repeat from * until you have completed the round. Step up through two cylinder beads to begin the next round.

6. Begin to add more silver charlottes using peyote stitch (see Techniques: Making a frilled collar bezel). Work the first herringbone stitch then pick up a silver charlotte, pass the needle through the charlotte from the last round and pick up another silver charlotte.

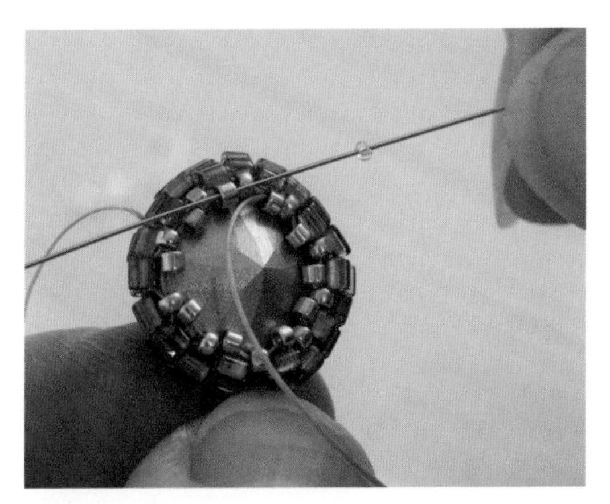

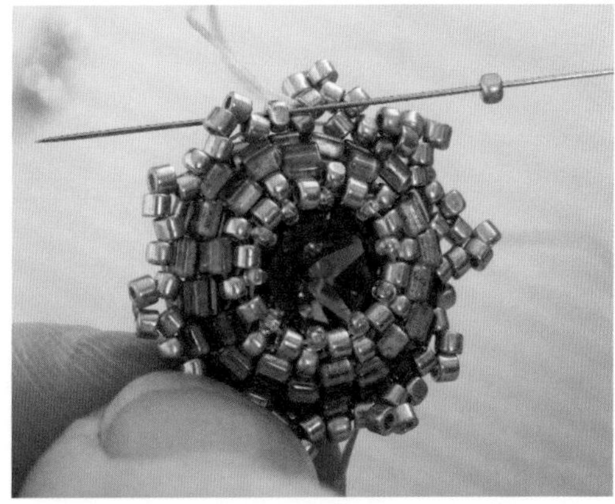

7. Take the needle through the next cylinder bead ready to work the next herringbone stitch. Continue all the way round and step up through two cylinder beads. On the next round add three charlottes in peyote stitch, and then four charlottes in the following round. Push all the silver peyote stitch sections forwards to shape the ring.

8. In the final round you will be embellishing the tips of herringbone stitch. After stepping up through two cylinder beads, pick up a cylinder bead, a silver charlotte and another cylinder bead. Go down through the next cylinder bead and work peyote stitch, adding five silver charlottes before the next herringbone stitch. Pull the thread taut as you go. Work all the way round. To finish, sew in the thread ends using half-hitch knots to secure and trim the ends neatly.

techniques ... making a plain bezel ... making a frilled collar bezel ... beader's knots

9. Glue the ring base to the reverse side.

bedazzled bezel brooch

Even plain bezels can look stunning. To create this fabulous brooch each crystal is surrounded by its own bezel. The crystals are then all stitched together securely, and a brooch pin adhered to the back. It is worth noting that larger stones may need more rounds to create a secure collar.

vibrant

1

gemstone wired cuff

Tucked inside the wire wraps of this super little bracelet are a bright mix of coloured stone beads. The beads are simply strung onto the wire, and then the wire is tightly wrapped around a blank cuff, making this the perfect wire project for those of you taking your first tentative steps with hard wire – don't worry, like all tough guys it's easy to manipulate once you know how!

you will need

- four orange stone chips
- two yellow stone chips
- four 3mm turquoise round beads
- four 6mm pink and jade round beads
- three 6mm purple round beads
- two 10mm green and turquoise flat faceted nuggets
- silver cuff blank
- 0.6mm (24swg/22awg) silver-coloured copper wire
- round-nose pliers
- flush cutters

If your budget allows, this would be the perfect project for gemstone beads. These can be purchased by the string.

1. Cut 1.5m (1½yd) of silver-coloured copper wire. Choose a focal bead from one of the larger beads; string it onto one end of the wire and slide it to the middle. Position the bead over the centre front of the cuff and tightly wrap each wire end around the back of the cuff.

2. Wrap the wire ends a second time around the cuff so there is a plain wire on each side of the focal bead. From this point, you'll work with just one wire end at a time; let the other end hang down until you're ready to complete the other side of the cuff.

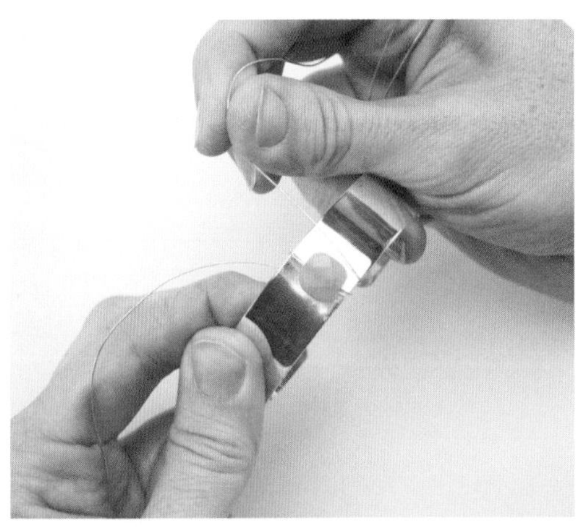

3. String a single round or stone chip onto the wire end you are working on. Slide the bead down the wire so it rests against the cuff. Tightly wrap the wire around the back of the cuff and then make an additional plain wire wrap. Continue tightly wrapping beads in this way, but make sure you leave the last quarter of the cuff uncovered, and leave the wire end hanging.

4. Now return to the other end of the wire and repeat step 3. Line up the stopping point with the other side, and to ensure good balance, carefully distribute colours, shapes and sizes of the beads across the front of the cuff.

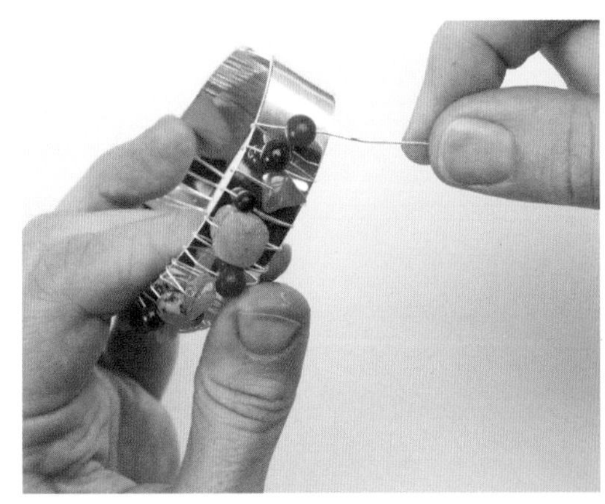

5. Working with one wire at a time, wrap the wire ends to cover the beads along the length of the beaded portion of the cuff, but without adding beads this time.

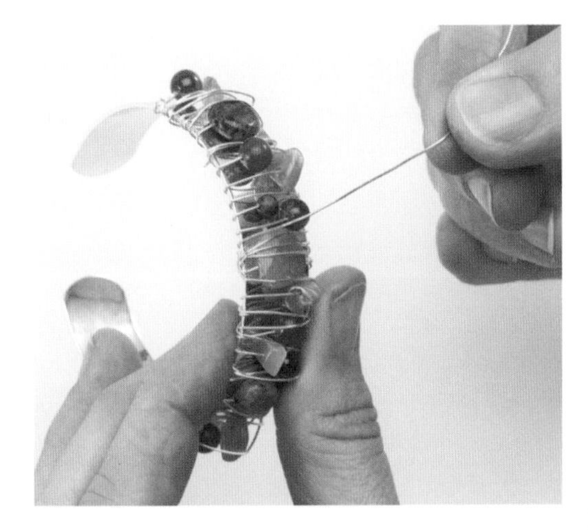

Try to avoid positioning the same kinds of beads alongside each other.

6. Use the round-nose pliers to bend the very end of the wire and tuck it into a bead. Repeat for the other wire end. If necessary, add a drop of jewellery glue to anchor the wire ends in place.

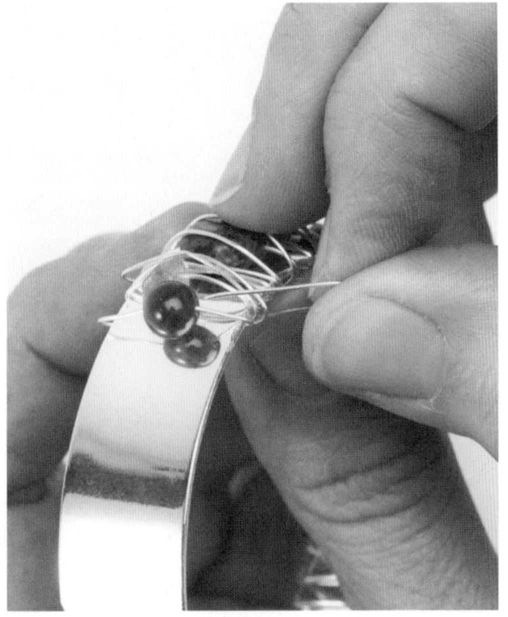

2

bright button necklace

This whimsical design gives new meaning to the expression one girl's rubbish is another girl's treasure. A selection of discarded keys and a pretty collection of bright retro buttons were used to make it, alongside little round beads in a variety of sizes and colours. Use the steps as a guide to create your own unique design. You could, for example, replace the metal keys with plastic Christmas cracker charms for a softer look.

you will need

- approx thirty 1.3cm (½in) plastic buttons
- four 2cm (⅞in) plastic buttons
- four 6mm round beads
- twelve 3mm round beads
- twenty-five 8mm white agate round beads
- three vintage metal keys
- one silver-plated spring ring clasp
- six 10mm silver-plated jump rings
- two 6mm silver-plated jump rings
- two silver-plated loop crimp ends
- 0.5mm (0.018in) satin copper beading wire
- 0.8mm (21swg/20awg) gunmetal enamelled wire
- 0.6mm (24swg/22awg) gunmetal enamelled wire
- round-nose pliers
- two pairs of chain-nose pliers
- wire cutters
- electric drill with 2mm (1⁄16in) bit
- two-hole punch
- permanent marker

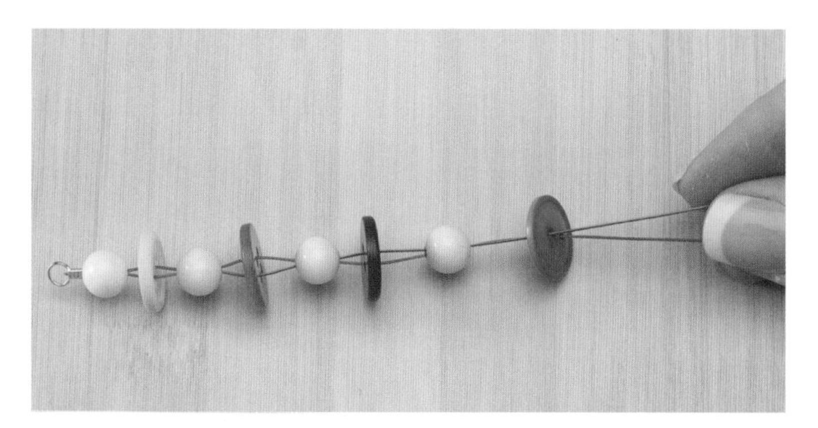

1. Cut two 61cm (24in) strands of satin copper beading wire; thread into a loop crimp and crimp with chain-nose pliers. String both wires through an agate bead. Thread each wire through a hole in a 1.3cm (½in) button. Thread another bead.

2. Alternate between buttons and beads until twenty-four buttons have been used, and end with an agate bead. Attach a loop crimp end and trim the excess wire.

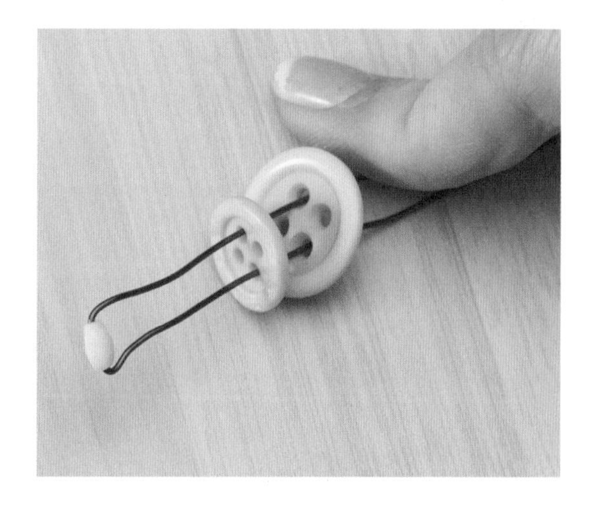

3. Cut a 20.5cm (8in) piece of 0.8mm (21swg/20awg) gunmetal enamelled wire. String a 6mm round bead onto the centre of the wire and bend both wire ends down. Thread the wire ends through a 1.3cm (½in) button, and then through a 2cm (⅞in) button.

4. Free-form wrap the wire ends into and around the button layers to secure them.

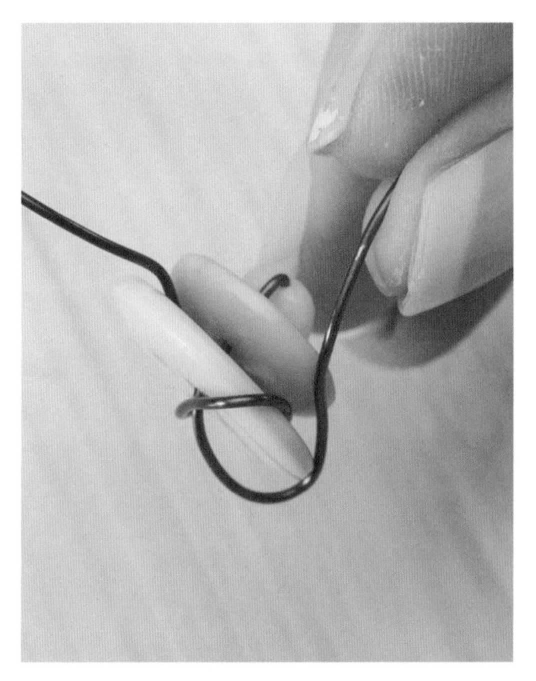

5. Secure the wire ends at the back of the button component by tucking them in with chain-nose pliers. Make four button components in all.

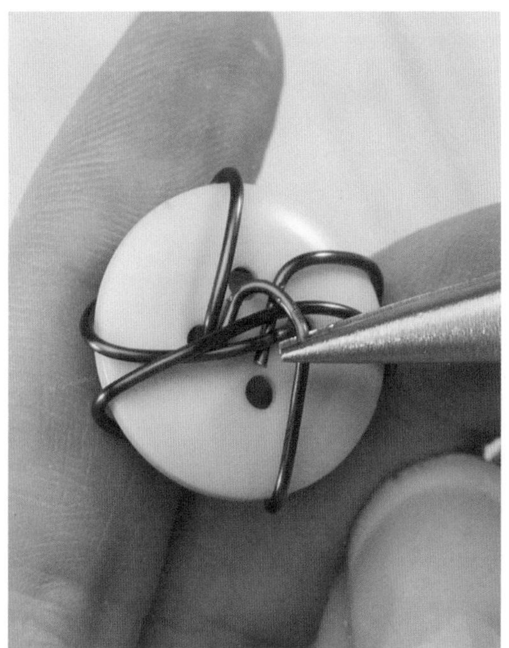

Choose buttons that have two or four holes in a variety of colours – the brighter the better.

6. Using the electric drill, drill a hole in the top of each button component.

7. Using a permanent marker, mark four dots equidistant along the top edges of a metal key. Drill four holes with the two-hole punch.

8. Cut a 20.5cm (8in) piece of 0.6mm (24swg/22awg) gunmetal enamelled wire. Place a 1.3cm (½in) button on top of the key and begin securing it with the wire, using the four drilled holes to weave from front to back and back to front. Twist and secure the wire ends with chain-nose pliers at the back.

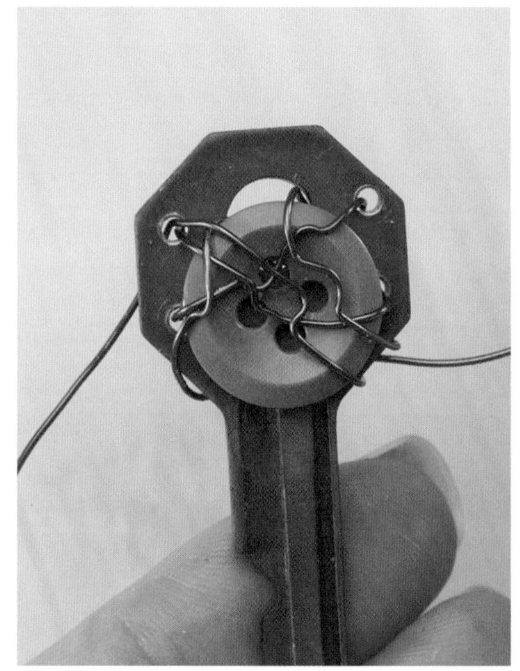

9. Wrap another 20.5cm (8in) piece of 0.6mm (24swg/22awg) wire tightly around the top of the base of the key. Cut off the excess wire and tuck in the tail. Working from the top of the base of the key, begin wrapping 0.6mm (24swg/22awg) wire around the key base, stringing on up to four 3mm beads. Secure the wire at the bottom, cut off the excess and tuck in the tail. Make another two button and key components.

10. Using the photograph as a guide, attach the button and key components with the 10mm jump rings, starting with a key embellishment in the centre of the necklace. Use the 6mm jump rings to attach half of a spring ring clasp fastener to the loop crimp ends at either end of the necklace.

techniques ... string, wire & chain ... essential tools ... wirework techniques

3

charming teacup bracelet

Visit a bead store and you will embark on a wonderful voyage of discovery. Alongside standard seeds and regular rounds, you are bound to find some sweet little novelties, like these wonderful lampwork teacup beads. This unusual charm bracelet provides plenty of opportunity for you to have a go at some exciting wirework techniques, including making the adorable crystal bead dangles.

you will need

- seven lampwork teacup beads
- thirty-two 4mm crystal rounds in a selection of colours
- sixteen 6mm x 9mm crystal tear drops
- thirty-two 3mm seamless sterling silver beads
- thirty-two 0.5mm (25swg/24awg) sterling silver headpins
- seven 0.6mm (24swg/22awg) sterling silver headpins
- four 6mm sterling silver jump rings
- toggle clasp
- 18cm (7in) of 6mm sterling silver rolo chain
- round-nose pliers
- two pairs of flat-nose pliers
- flush cutters

1. Attach the two parts of the toggle clasp to either end of the chain with two jump rings (see Techniques: Opening and closing a jump ring). Look out for unusual fastenings – this sterling silver teapot and spoon toggle clasp was the perfect choice for the teacup charm bracelet.

2. Sandwich a teacup bead between two round crystal beads on a 0.6mm (24swg/22awg) headpin, and wire wrap this dangle to the fourth link of the chain (see Techniques: Making a wrapped loop). Repeat, adding a teacup dangle to every fourth link in the chain. Wire wrap all of the dangles to the same side of the chain so that they hang properly.

3. Now add the teardrop dangles. Slide a sterling silver bead and a teardrop bead (with the thin end towards the silver bead) onto a 0.5mm (25swg/24awg) headpin. Wire wrap this dangle to the first link of the chain. Continue adding teardrop dangles every two links.

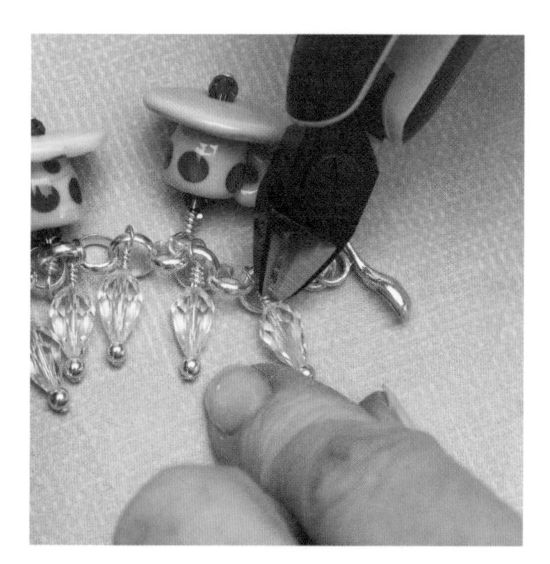

4. Now make the round crystal dangles. Slide a sterling silver bead and a crystal round onto a 0.5mm (25swg/24awg) headpin and wire wrap the headpin to the first link, opposite the first teardrop dangle. Repeat every two links to the end of the bracelet.

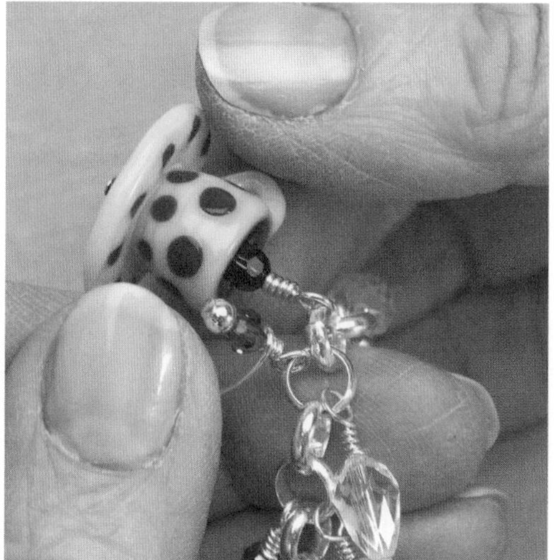

techniques ... essential tools ... wirework techniques

2

polka-dot necklace

It couldn't be easier to make your own beads using rolled up strips of fabric. Barrel beads can be made from a printed cotton to match your favourite top, or you can choose a plain fabric and embellish it with a simple polka-dot pattern using acrylic paint. The result is a great necklace ideal for that big night out.

you will need

- three 3cm (1in) glass focus beads
- size 8 matt black seed beads
- size 11 white seed beads
- two crimp beads
- beading wire
- toggle clasp
- cotton fabric
- white acrylic paint
- gloss acrylic glazing liquid
- heavy gel
- paintbrush
- mandrels (or bamboo skewers)
- crimp pliers
- wire cutters

1. Cut ten strips of your chosen fabric measuring 3 x 13cm (1⅛ x 5in) and eight strips measuring 1.3 x 13cm (½ x 5in). Paint a thin layer of acrylic glazing liquid on the first 3–5cm (1–2in) of the back of the fabric strip.

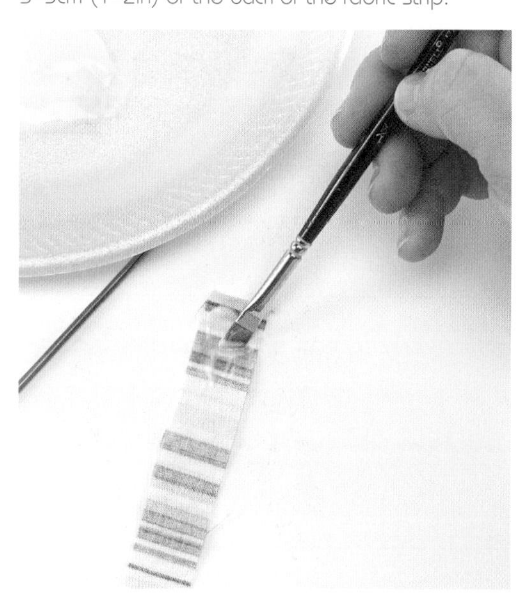

2. Tuck the coated end of the fabric strip tightly to the mandrel. Carefully start to roll the fabric strip around the mandrel.

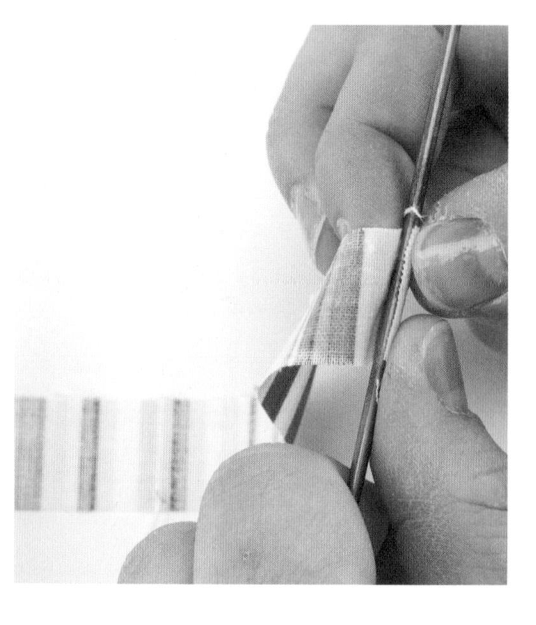

To remove the beads from the mandrels, carefully twist them to loosen, then twist and pull upward at the same time. If you pull straight up, you could pull the centre fabric out of the bead.

3. Continue to roll the fabric strip until you reach the portion of the fabric strip not coated with glazing liquid. Brush glazing liquid onto the uncoated portion of the fabric strip and continue to roll until the strip is completely wrapped around the mandrel.

4. Brush another coat of glazing liquid on the finished bead. Let the bead dry completely. Add a second coat of glazing liquid to the bead and let it dry once more. Apply two to three coats of the heavy gel to the rolled bead. Let each coat dry before adding the next coat. Remove the dry bead from the mandrel and trim any frayed threads from the edges of the bead using a small pair of scissors.

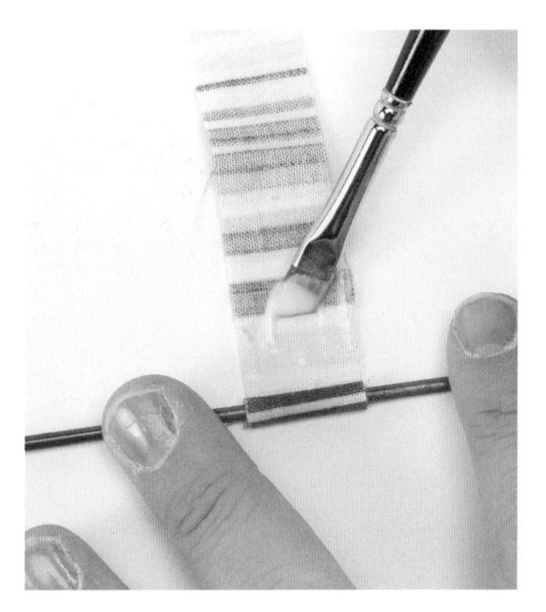

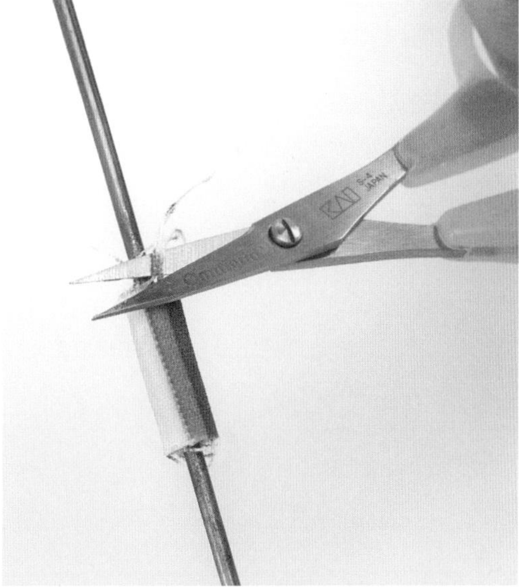

5. If you have made your barrel beads from plain fabric, decorate them with a polka-dot pattern before removing them from the mandrels. Use white acrylic paint and space the dots evenly over the surface. Let the paint dry. Add another coat of heavy gel to each bead. Let the gel dry before removing the beads from the mandrels. You should have ten 3cm (1⅛in) and eight 1.3cm (½in) beads.

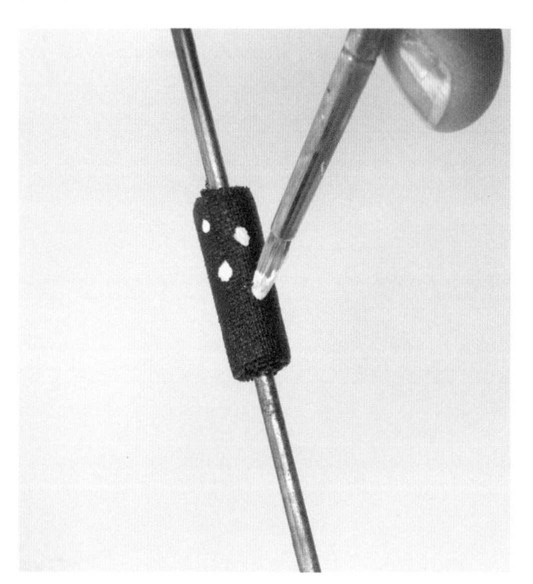

6. Cut a piece of beading wire 76cm (30in) long. Slide a crimp bead onto the wire about 10cm (4in) from one end. Add on the bar end of the toggle clasp and loop the wire through the crimp bead once again. Use crimp pliers to close the crimp bead in place.

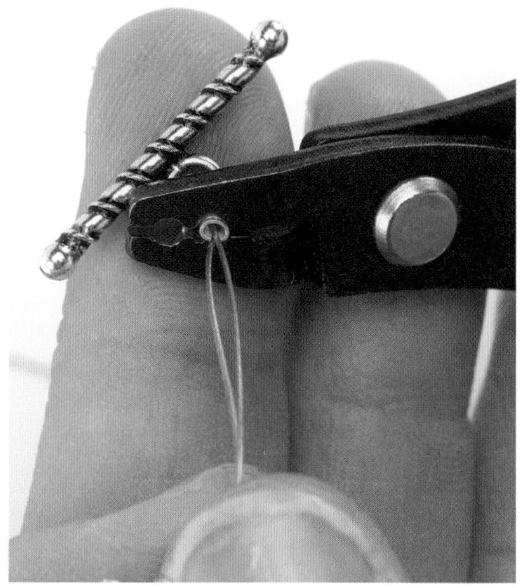

7. String the beads onto the beading wire in the following sequence: black seed bead, white seed bead, black seed bead, large fabric bead, black seed bead, white seed bead, black seed bead, small fabric bead. Repeat this beading pattern three more times.

8. To make the centre section of the necklace, string the beads onto the wire in the following sequence: black/white/black seed beads, glass focus bead, black/white/black seed beads, large fabric bead, black/white/black seed beads, glass focus bead, black/white/black seed beads, large fabric bead, black/white/black seed beads, glass focus bead, black/white/black seed beads.

9. Repeat step 7 in reverse to finish stringing the necklace. Slide the remaining crimp bead onto the beading wire. Add on the loop end of the toggle clasp, loop the wire back through the crimp bead, and close the crimp bead in place. Thread the extra wire at each end through the first few beads for added strength and use wire cutters to trim the excess wire.

techniques ... findings & fastenings ... essential tools

ocean swirl ring

This project is for those who need instant gratification. In just a few minutes, you can wrap and twist a length of wire around a single lampwork flower bead to create a beautiful show-stopping ring. The trick is to find a low-profile bead that will sit flat against your hand with a large enough opening to accommodate a double thickness of 1.0mm (19swg/18awg) wire. Happy hunting!

you will need

- 1.0mm (19swg/18awg) silver-coloured wire
- centre-drilled lampwork flower bead
- ring mandrel
- chain-nose pliers
- flush cutters

Lampwork beads are handmade with rods or canes of plain or patterned glass using a blowtorch, so although the production process can be replicated, no two beads are ever identical.

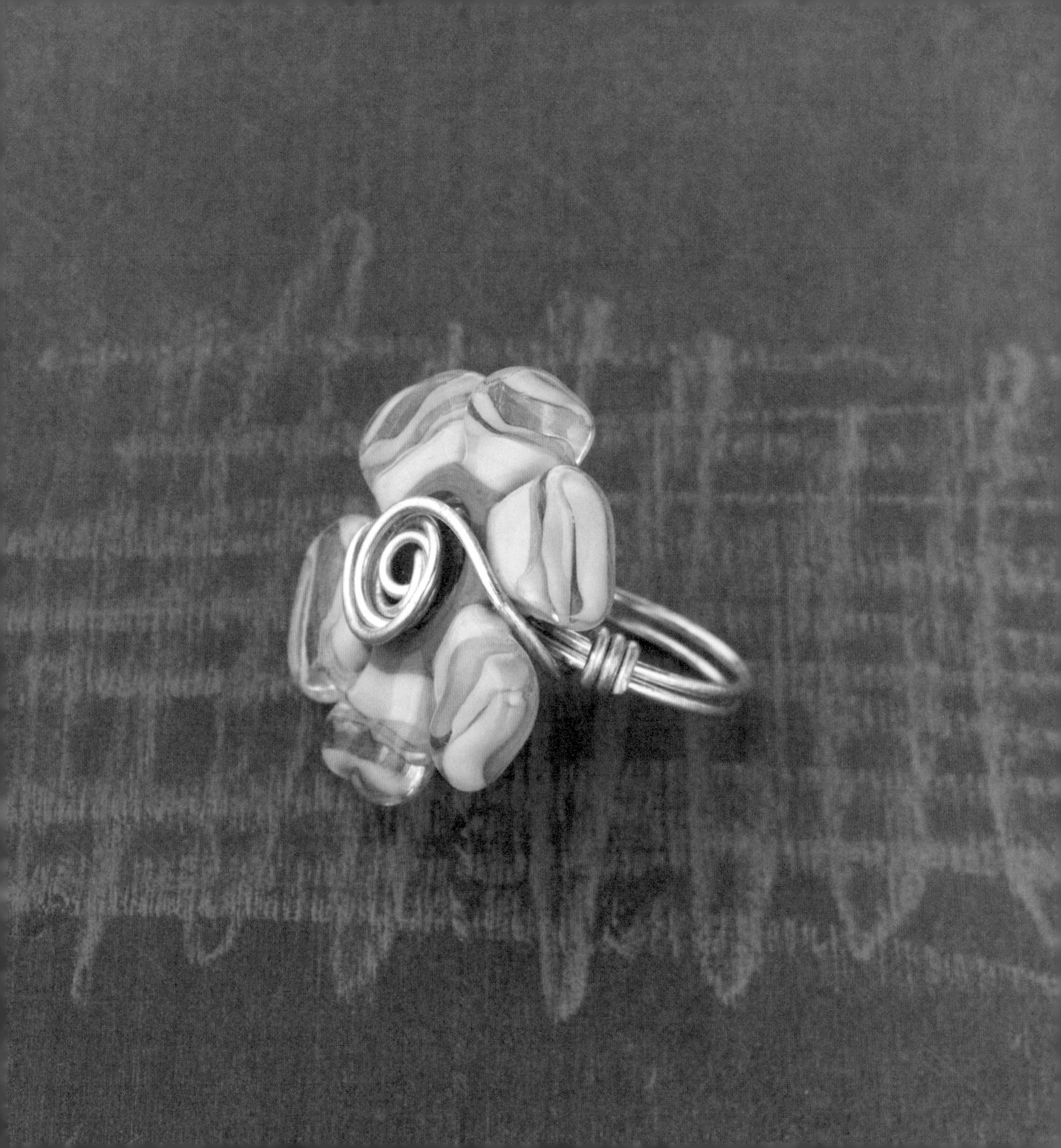

1. To determine your ring size, slide a favourite ring onto the mandrel and mark the position, using tape on a metal mandrel or pen on a wooden one. Cut a 40.5cm (16in) length of wire. Wrap the centre of the wire completely around the marked section of the mandrel and then bring both wire ends back around to the front to make a double-banded ring. Use the chain-nose pliers to bend the wires to a 90-degree angle where they meet.

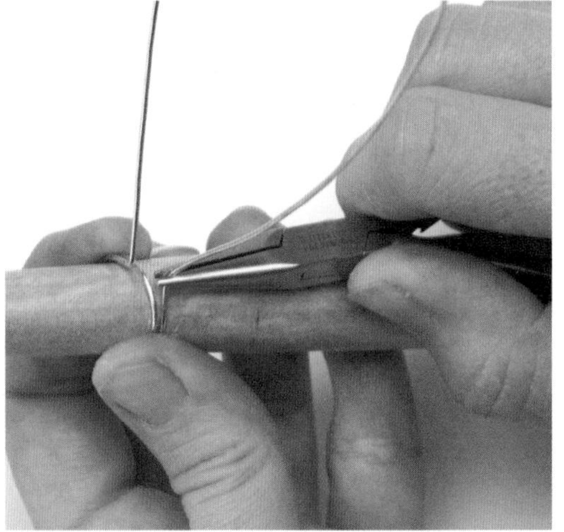

2. Slide the lampwork bead onto both wires so it rests directly on top of the ring band.

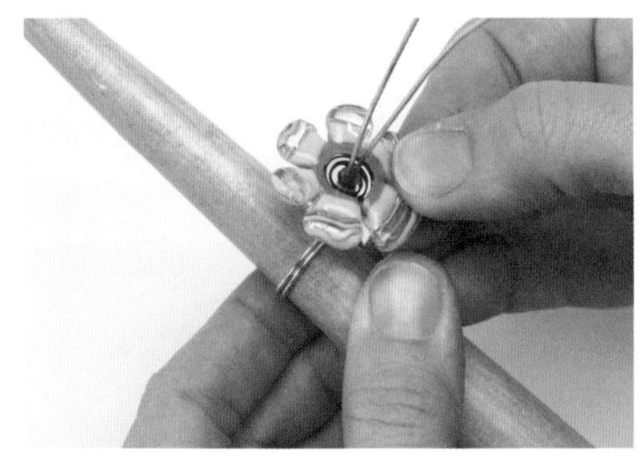

3. Holding both wires together between finger and thumb, rotate them twice around the centre of the bead to form a spiral.

4. Separate the wires. Thread one through a break in the petals on the left side and the other wire through a break in the petals on the right side.

5. Slide the ring off the mandrel. Tightly wrap each wire two to three times around the double ring band. Trim the wires with flush cutters, and use chain-nose pliers to press the cut wire ends flat against the ring band.

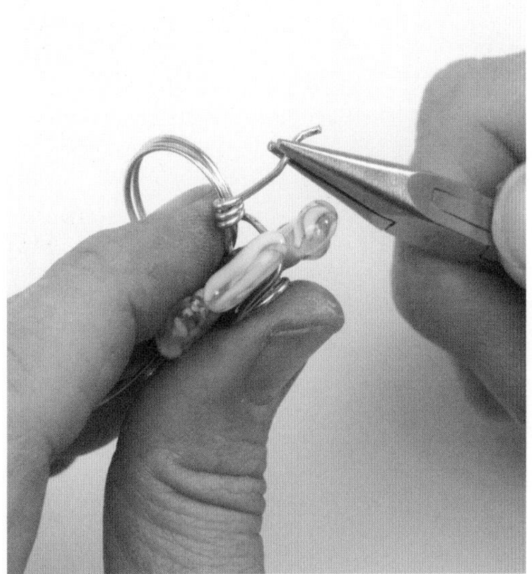

be inspired

1

love macramé bracelet

Macramé is a versatile knotting technique very much of the moment in the seventies – think macramé hanging plant holders! Thankfully you can just as easily use it to create stunning knotted necklaces and bracelets from hemp cord, which is available in a rainbow of colours. If you are a macramé virgin, this project is perfect for you as it requires just one simple knot.

you will need

- five flat metal beads
- one round glass bead
- 4.6m (5yd) of 1mm blue hemp cord
- jewellery glue

Make sure that the beads you choose have holes that are large enough to accommodate multiple strands of the hemp cord. The finished length of this bracelet is 19cm (7½in).

1. Cut one strand of 92cm (1yd) and two strands of 1.83m (2yd) from the hemp cord. Fold each strand in half and tie the centres of all three together in an overhand knot to make a loop (see Techniques: Tying an overhand knot with a loop).

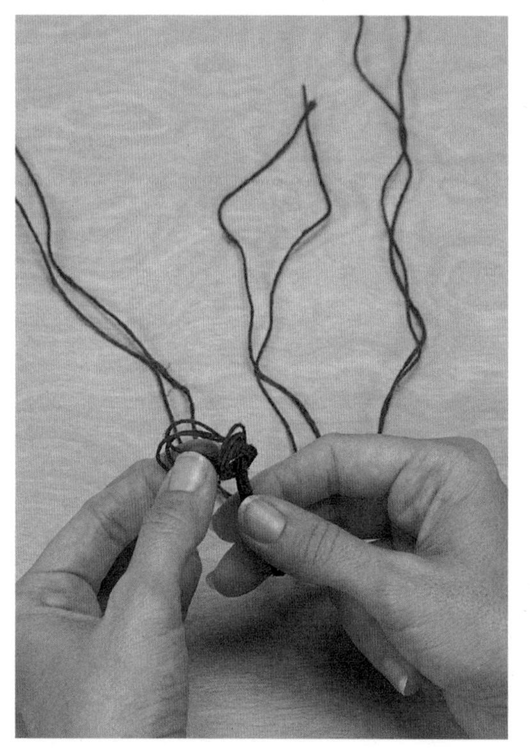

2. Organize the strands, positioning the two shorter lengths in the centre with two long strands on either side. Make a square knot. The first part of this is to fold the two left strands over the centre strands. Bring the two right strands over the left stands, thread them under the centre strands and up through the loop in the left strands. Pull evenly on both ends to tighten the first half of the square knot and slide it up under the overhand knot.

3. To complete the square knot, fold the right strands over the centre strands. Bring the left strands over the right strands, thread them under the centre strands and up through the loop in the right strands. Pull evenly on the ends to tighten the second half of the knot and position it under the first half. Make another seven square knots.

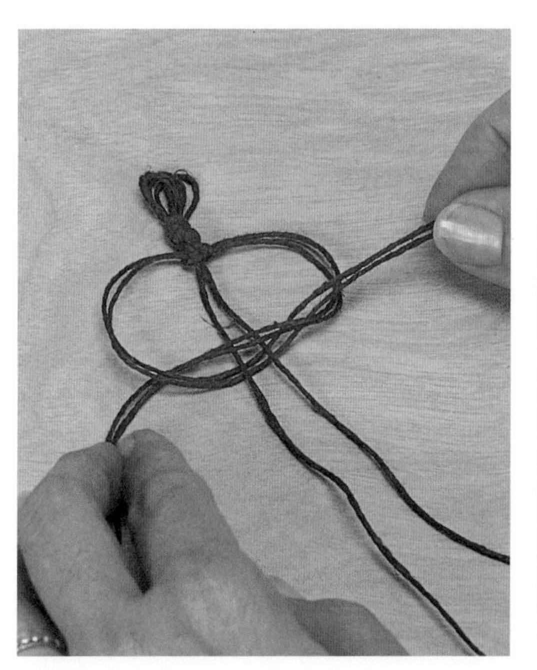

4. Put glue on the ends of the two centre strands of hemp to prevent fraying. Thread both centre strands through a flat metal bead; slide the bead up under the last square knot. Follow the bead with another square knot.

5. Thread another flat metal bead onto the two centre strands and push it up under the last square knot. Repeat the process to string three more beads separated by single square knots.

6. Follow the last bead with eight more square knots. Tie all six strands into an overhand knot (see Techniques: Overhand knot), then thread all the ends through a round glass bead. Tie all the strands in a second overhand knot to secure the bead and then trim the ends. To fasten the bracelet, thread the knotted-bead end through the starting loop made in step 1.

techniques ... beader's knots

macramé marvels

By simply changing colours and beads, each macramé design takes on a different look. For example, for great summertime jewellery use natural-coloured hemp and drilled shell beads. To make a choker, extend the length of the piece to 34cm (13½in).

korean maedeup earrings

Maedeup (pronounced mae-doop) is the traditional craft of decorative knotwork popular in Korea where these colourful trimmings adorn not only jewellery but clothes and accessories in abundance. With about thirty-three basic knots to choose from, the embellishing possibilities are endless. The knotting does require a little practise, but these ethnic-inspired earrings will give you a good reason to learn your first three maedeup – the dorae, the saengjjok and the sanjeongja.

you will need

- two sterling silver Chinese coin charms
- two silver earring wires
- 92cm (1yd) of 1mm green hemp cord
- two pairs of flat-nose pliers
- leather crafting awl
- small embroidery scissors
- instant bond glue

The best way to determine if cording is suitable for maedeup is to test it out with a few maedeup to see what it looks like and how it is to work with.

乾隆通寶

1. Cut the cord in half. Thread an earring wire onto each cord (to open the earring wire loop, see Techniques: Opening and closing a jump ring) and fold the cord in half. Keep the earring wire near the fold and make a dorae maedeup 1cm (⅜in) from the fold. Continue with a saengjjok maedeup.

2. Make a sanjeongja maedeup. Thread a coin onto both cords. Make a dorae maedeup. Loop around the **two** cords coming down from the saengjjok maedeup (instead of the usual one cord). Finish as for a regular dorae maedeup and tighten, leaving a 5mm (3⁄16in) loop. Using the awl, begin tightening at the start of the maedeup; follow the cord around the maedeup, keeping the shape of the maedeup as you go. You are aiming for a symmetrical effect.

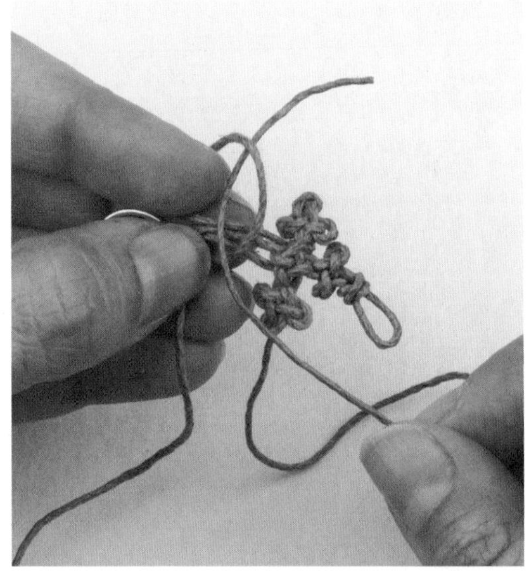

3. Cut off the excess cord and glue the end to prevent it from fraying. Repeat to make a second earring.

the maedeup

There are just three maedeup to master. When practising, it can help to use two different coloured cords, as this makes it easier to see the path of the maedeup; when working with two cords, knot them together before you begin.

The dorae or double connection knot

The saengjjok or cloverleaf knot

The sanjeongja or three-character knot

techniques ... findings & fastenings ... opening and closing a jump ring

tying a dorae

1. Using two cords, loop the purple cord around the pink cord. Anchor the loop with your left thumb and index finger.

2. Thread the purple cord all the way through the loop.

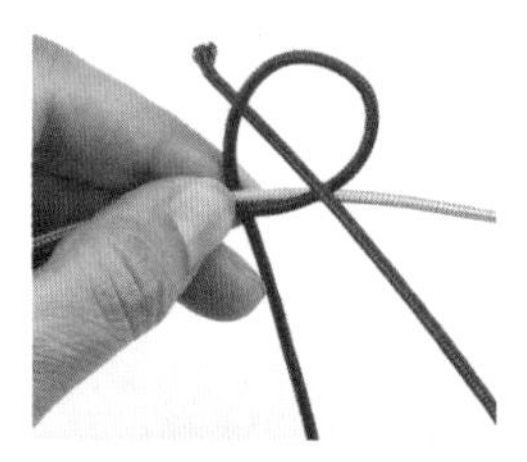

3. Pull the purple cord from the base of the loop to move the loop from the top to the bottom of the cord.

4. Loop the pink cord around the purple cord to create a second loop. Anchor the pink loop to the left of the base of the purple loop with your left index finger and thumb.

5. Thread the pink cord through both loops. Gently pull the purple cord from the right side until the maedeup is tightened and then repeat with the pink cord.

Right-handers: keep the cord anchored with your left thumb and index finger, and use your right thumb and index finger to loop, thread and pull (left-handers, reverse this).

tying a saengjjok

1. Make a loop and anchor it with your left thumb and index finger.

2. Loop the right cord around the base of the loop and pinch it with your right thumb and index finger.

3. Release your left hand and make a loop with the left cord.

4. Thread the left loop through the right loop.

5. Use your right middle finger to anchor the loop to the top of your right index finger. Use your left hand to pull the left cord at the bottom of the loop.

6. The loop will now be under where it was originally.

7. Use your left fingers to move the loop you were holding with your right fingers, centring it over the cord and lower loop that you were holding in your right fingers.

8. Use your right fingers to take the right cord and thread it down into the top of the loop.

9. Continue under the two cords and back over the loop.

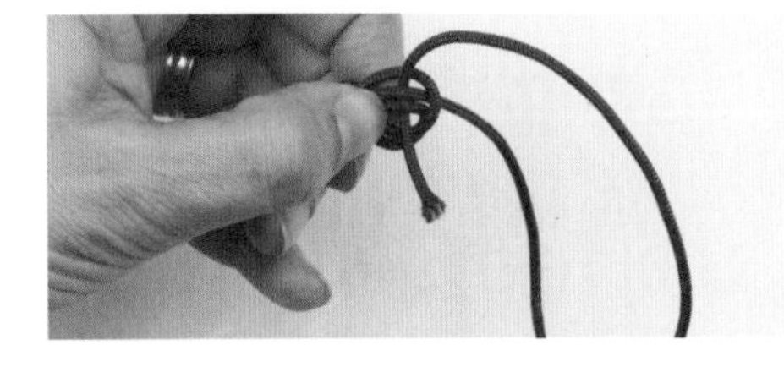

10. Pull the two parallel cords on each side.

11. Pull the knot tight. Now you will have three loops.

12. To tighten, use an awl and start at one of the side loops and follow the cord around. Continue until all three loops are tightened. Press the awl into each loop to enlarge to finish.

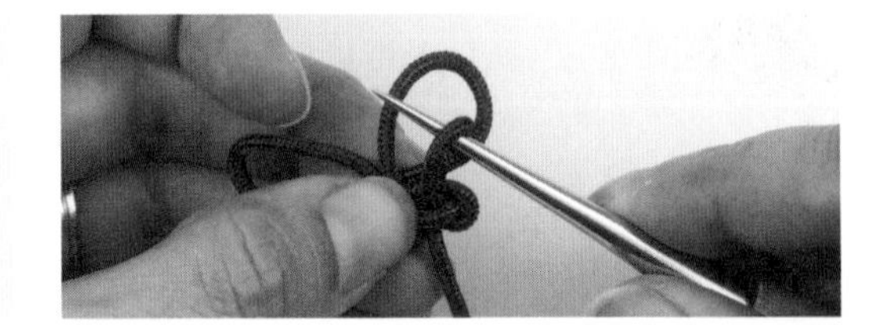

tying a sanjeongja

1. This knot is created by joining three saengjjok. Using two cords, make and tighten a saengjjok on each cord (see Tying a saengjjok), leaving at least 5cm (2in) from the base of the cord.

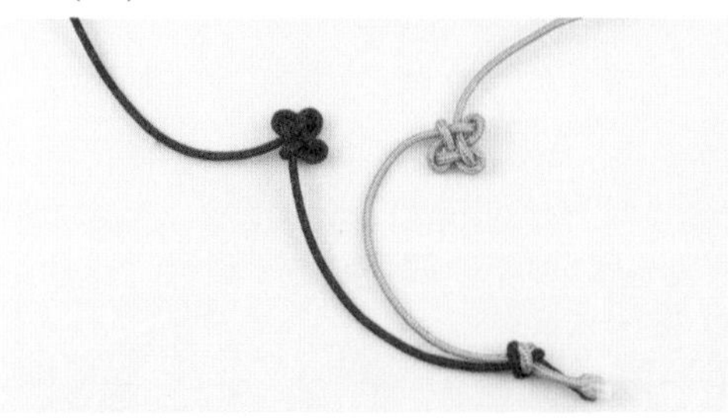

2. Make a loop with the purple cord on the right side of the purple saengjjok and anchor it with your left thumb and index finger. Loop the pink cord around the base of the purple loop and pinch it with your right thumb and index finger.

3. Make a loop with the purple cord to the left of the purple saengjjok.

4. Thread this loop through the right purple loop.

5. Use the right middle finger to anchor the loop to the top of your right index finger. Use your left hand to pull the left cord at the bottom of the loop. The loop is now under where it was originally.

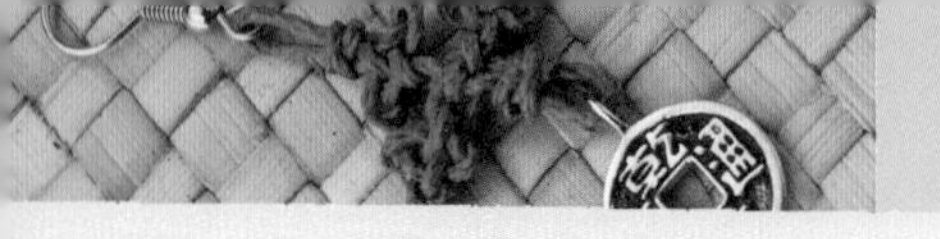

6. Use your left fingers to move the purple loop you were holding with your right fingers to the right. Centre the loop over the two pink cords that you were holding in your right fingers.

7. Use your right fingers to take the pink cord and thread it down into the top of the loop. Continue under the two pink cords and back up through the loop.

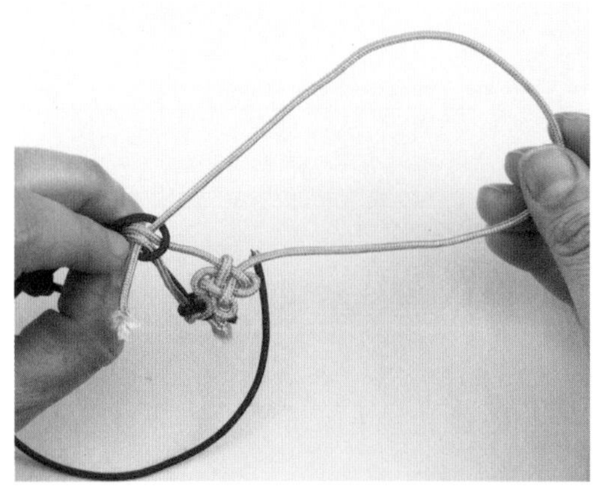

8. Pull the two parallel cords on the left (purple) and right (pink) sides. Pull them tight.

9. You will have three loops. Use your fingers to tighten everything.

10. Turn this so the cord ends are facing away from you. Place your awl into the left cord of the purple saengjjok and loosen it so you can get a grip on the cord.

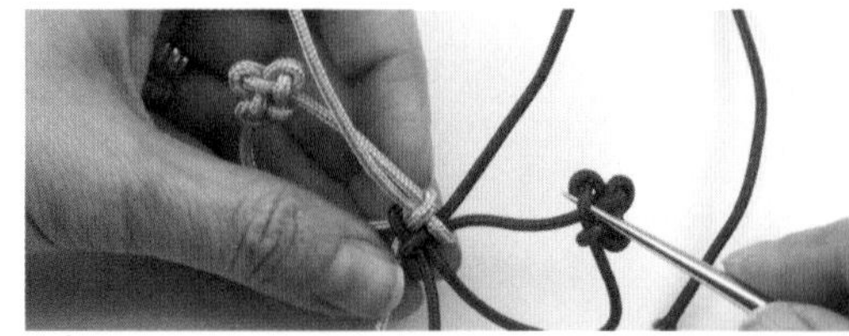

11. Use your right index finger and thumb to pull the cord while securing the centre knot with your left hand: pull until the purple saengjjok is tight against the centre knot.

12. Tighten as you would a regular saengjjok. Place the awl into the right cord of the centre knot.

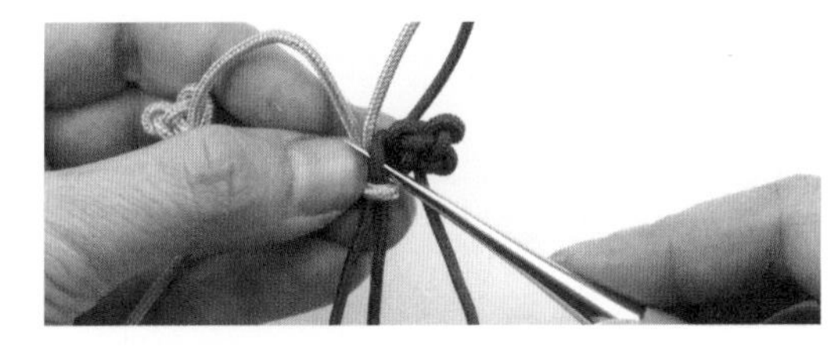

13. You are now ready to tighten.

14. Pull the purple cord end to tighten.

15. Place the awl into the right cord of the pink saengjjok.

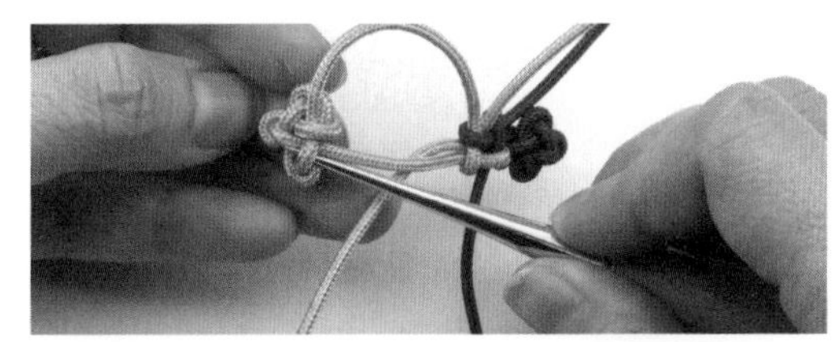

16. Continue tightening the pink saengjjok as you did the purple.

sparkly flower ring

With just a little bit of wool roving, hot water and a little soap you can make a beautiful felt bead – the process is very simple and can be completed in almost no time at all. The finished beads can be cut in half to make pretty little rings that will be very much admired by your friends, so make several!

you will need

- small piece of wool roving
- embellishments: beads, sew-on gems and ric-rac scraps
- wool felt scrap
- ring blank
- sewing needle and thread
- tacky glue
- jewellery glue
- scallop-edge scissors
- scissors

Wool roving can be bought in 25g (1oz) weights, which will be sufficient to make quite a number of beads. It is available in a stunning array of colours.

1. Make a 2cm (⅞in) felt ball bead (see Techniques: Making a felt ball bead). Cut the felted bead in half with a pair of sharp scissors. Using a pair of scallop-edge scissors, mark and cut out a circle base from a scrap of wool felt, just a little larger than the diameter of the felted bead.

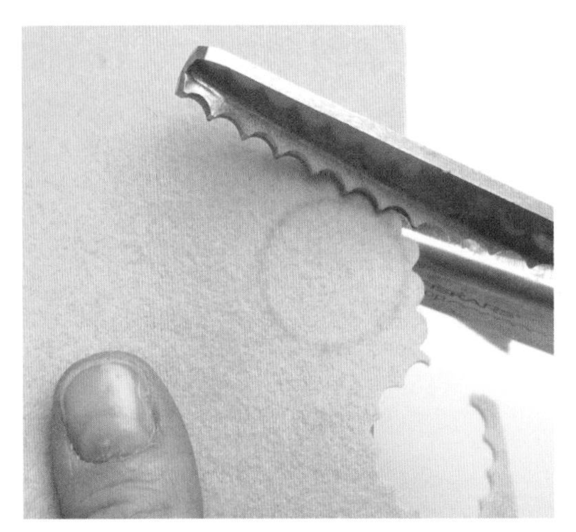

When cutting out the felt base, line up the point of the scallop with the edge of the circle.

2. Glue the half bead onto the felt circle using tacky glue and let it dry. Sew on your selected embellishments; tie off and clip the thread ends.

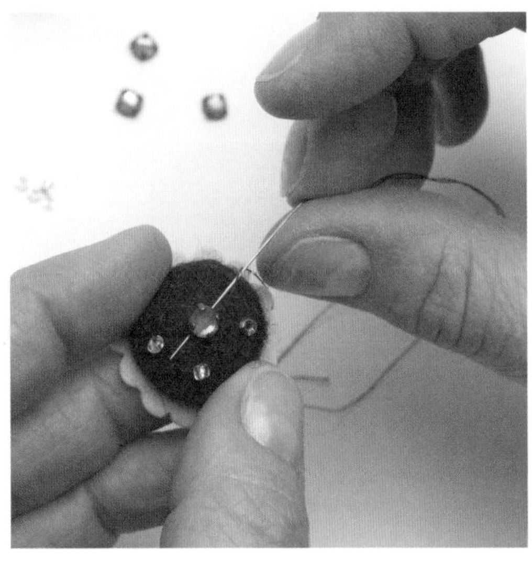

3. Use jewellery glue to adhere the felt flower to a ring blank, and let it dry.

a handful of rings

These sweet little rings are so easy to make you will want to make more than one. You can have such fun adorning them with bits of narrow ric-rac, tiny flower beads and decorative stitching. Here are just a few ideas to inspire you.

techniques **...** findings & fastenings ... making a felt ball bead

twilight necklace

Once started, felt ball bead making is hopelessly addictive, and this gorgeous pendant necklace gives you the opportunity to make lots of them. The pendant's shape and colour has been chosen to complement the little felt wonders, which are strung in alternating colours and separated by silver seed beads. Reminiscent of a starry night, this would make the perfect party accessory.

you will need

- fourteen black felt ball beads
- fourteen purple felt ball beads
- size 6 silver seed beads
- disk pendant with a bail
- toggle clasp
- beading cord
- size 11 straw needle
- awl
- scissors
- jeweller's glue

1. Use the awl to make a hole through each felt ball bead. Cut a piece of beading cord measuring 76cm (30in); tie to half of the clasp using an overhand knot and leaving a 5cm (2in) tail. Add a little jeweller's glue to the knot and let it dry completely.

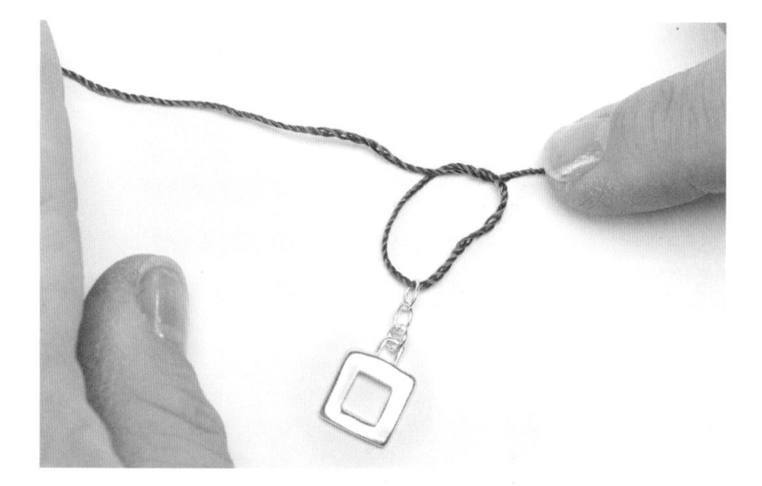

2. Starting with a silver seed bead, begin stringing the beads, alternating felt beads with seed beads.

3. After stringing twelve felt ball beads, string three seed beads in a row. Slide the disk pendant over the three seed beads.

4. String the second half of the necklace. Tie the other half of the clasp to the end of the beading cord and secure the knot with jeweller's glue. Using the straw needle, sew the bead cord tails into the beads and trim off.

techniques ... making a felt ball bead ... beader's knots

2

asian-inspired earrings

Although there is a multitude of ready-made beads, charms and pendants available to you, it can be great fun to make your own, and one of the easiest ways is to use polymer clay. The clay can be cut to any shape you desire, stamped and embellished, and then baked to harden. These elegant earrings give you the perfect opportunity to explore this versatile material for yourself.

you will need

- two 8mm black glass round beads
- two 10mm black glass elongated oval-shaped beads with vertical hole
- four 6mm antique gold jump rings
- two antique gold earring wires
- two headpins
- polymer clay: translucent and red
- embossing powders: black and old paper distress
- clear embossing ink pad
- translucent liquid clay
- branches with leaves rubber stamp
- oval cutter
- handheld heat gun
- ceramic tile
- craft knife
- slicing blade
- needle-nose pliers
- instant bond glue

1. The clay needs to be conditioned by rolling between the palms of your hands so that it is soft enough to shape easily. Condition a ¼ cube of translucent clay and flatten it to a thick pad. To mix the distress embossing powder into the clay, add a 1.25ml (¼ teaspoon) and fold the edges of the clay inward around the powder; knead the clay until the speckles are distributed evenly.

2. Flatten the clay to a little less than 3mm (⅛in). Cut out two ovals for the earring bases and remove the excess clay from around the shapes. Bake following the manufacturer's instructions and allow to cool.

Work directly onto a ceramic tile to avoid having to move the clay to bake it.

3. Working on a piece of card that has been folded in half and using the clear embossing ink, stamp the design onto the earring bases. Sprinkle black embossing powder over the stamped design and tap the back of the clay to dislodge any excess (the folded card allows this to be easily poured back into the container). Using a handheld heat gun, heat the design until it becomes slightly raised and shiny.

4. Turn the ovals over and press the top ridges onto the stamp pad to create a border of ink around the shapes. Emboss as in step 3.

Remove any stray particles from the clay with the tip of a cotton bud.

5. To add a bezel, flatten a sheet of conditioned red pearl polymer clay to a little less than 2mm (1/16in) thick. Place the decorated ovals right side up on the red clay and loosely cut around them to leave a 6mm (1/4in) border. Remove the excess clay. Apply a thin layer of translucent liquid clay around the borders and fold up against the earring bases. Using a slicing blade, trim away the excess bezel clay to sit flush with the stamped oval. Lightly smooth the cut ridge with your fingertip.

6. Add a loop to the top and bottom edges of the decorated ovals. Using the needle-nose pliers, grasp a jump ring on the opposite side of the closed ends; add a dot of instant bond glue to the ends and press halfway into the centre edge of the clay, just below the baked layer. Press the back of the bezel to secure the clay around the ring. Bake.

7. Make two earring dangles (see Techniques: Making a plain loop), and secure to the jump ring at the bottom of each oval; attach an earring wire to the top jump ring.

red rock necklace

For a pendant necklace to match, make a larger oval-shaped bead as well as a rugby-shaped bead and join together. Strands of irregular-cut red rock stone chips look great against the black glass beads.

techniques ... making a plain loop ... opening and closing a jump ring

3

strawberry-thief bracelet

Design and make your very own patterned tile beads by introducing inkjet t-shirt transfer paper to polymer clay – somebody really should have done it sooner. The result is a beautifully sculpted bracelet that will not fail to impress. We have chosen a William Morris inspired image which is baked onto the clay and cooled, then colour-tinted with pastel chalks. What design will you choose?

you will need

- size 6 black glass seed beads
- thin strong elastic cord, black or clear
- polymer clay: white and black
- translucent liquid clay
- iron-on inkjet t-shirt transfer paper for light fabrics
- soft pastel chalk sticks
- fantastix applicators
- cocktail stick (toothpick)
- transparent ruler
- extra-fine mist spray bottle
- scissors
- acrylic bead roller
- two ceramic tiles
- slicing blade
- varnishing glaze
- jewellery glue

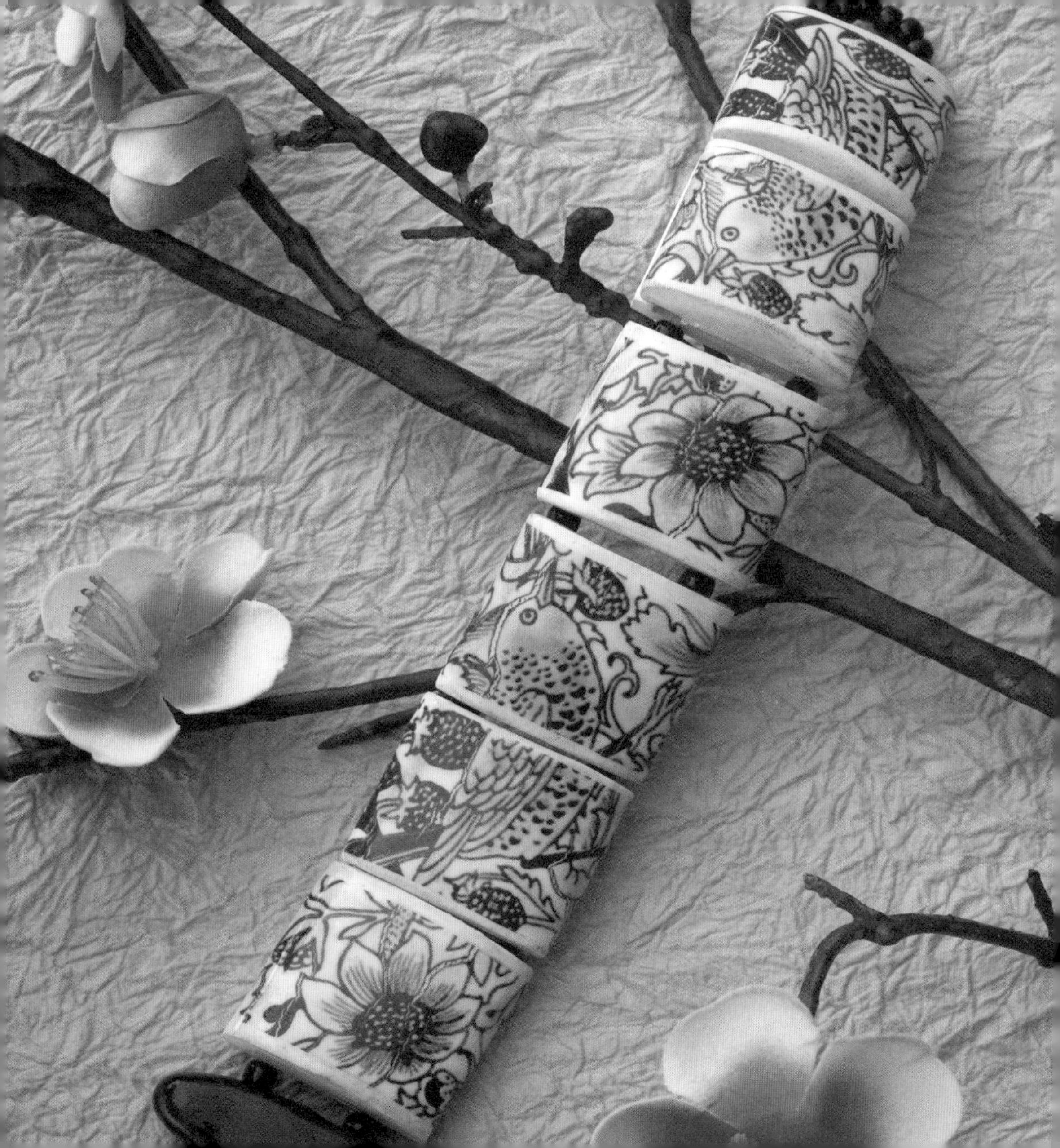

1. First decide on the length of your bracelet. Measure your wrist and add 4cm (1½in) so the bracelet will move freely. From this total length, calculate how many 3cm (1in) wide tiles you will need to make.

2. Print your chosen image onto transfer paper on an inkjet printer using the best quality setting. Cut out a 4 x 2cm (1½ x ⅞in) piece of card for the tile template, and use to trace off areas of the design. Set the image aside to allow the ink to dry.

3. Form a smooth ball using a ½ cube of white clay. Roll the ball into a 2cm (⅝in) thick rope of clay measuring approx 13cm (5in). Mist the acrylic bead roller oval trough with water and press the clay rope into the shape. Trim the overlapping ends with the slicing blade. Remove the clay and secure to a ceramic tile, flat side down.

If you're making six or seven tiles, roll a short 2cm (⅝in) rope to cut extra bead(s).

4. Place a transparent ruler up against the edge of the clay strip. Trim it to measure 13cm (5in) long. Cut the clay into five pieces 3cm (1in) long.

5. Cut out the selected areas of the design just inside the traced line. Remove the transfer from its paper backing and place over a clay tile to centre it over the rounded edges. Smooth, gently rubbing from the centre outward and press the ends around to the back of the clay tile.

6. Now make the bottom two bead layers. Roll a ½ cube of conditioned white clay to 2mm (1/16in) thick, making a long strip that measures at least 30cm (12in) for a five-tile bracelet (36cm/14in for six tiles; 41cm/16in for seven tiles). Cut the strip in half and place on a ceramic tile. Using the slicing blade, cut a 1cm (3/8in) wide strip down the centre of one sheet, lift and place it horizontally in the centre of the second sheet. Lift the remaining two clay pieces and place them on the second sheet, 5mm (3/16in) away from the centre strip, to form two channels. Apply an even coat of translucent liquid clay to the top strips. Avoid getting the liquid into the channels. The liquid will act as glue during the baking cycle to tightly secure the layers together.

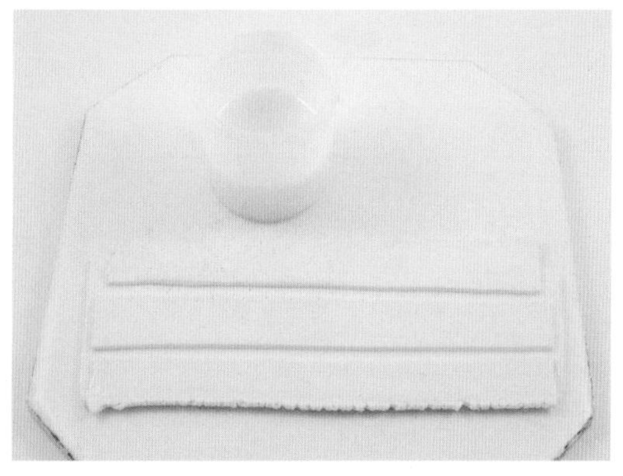

7. Press the transfer beads onto the layered strips, centring them over the two channels. Cut away the excess clay from around all four sides of the beads using a slicing blade. Check the sides of the beads to make sure the holes will easily accommodate the cording.

8. Roll a smooth 2cm (5/8in) ball of black clay and shape it so it's tapered at both ends. Pierce two holes through the toggle bead, 6mm (1/4in) apart.

9. Bake the clay tile beads and toggle bead, following the manufacturer's guidance for clay thickness. When completely cool, check to make sure the elastic cord fits through all of the holes, and enlarge the holes with a drill if required. Squeeze the bead layers together as you slowly drill by hand.

10. Use the applicator sticks to colour tint the transfer images. Rub the applicator stick against the side edge of a chalk stick to pick up colour, then apply the colour inside the designs. When the designs are complete, tint the background and the remaining white areas of the beads fuchsia pink. Varnish the decorated tile beads with two or more coats of a polymer-clay friendly glaze.

11. To assemble the bracelet, thread ten seed beads onto the centre of a 61cm (24in) length of elastic cord. Thread each tile (except the last one), placing one seed bead between them.

12. To add the last tile, thread the elastic through a seed bead and then through the top hole of the tile. Add another seed bead. Thread the elastic up into the right hole of the toggle bead and then down through the left hole. Add a seed bead, then thread through the bottom hole of the tile. Tie a reef (square) knot in the cord ends, add a dot of jewellery glue to the knot and gently pull it into the second tile bead hole to conceal it.

techniques ... beader's knots

cute retro bracelet

Buttons make great focus beads, and when covered with fabric, the result can be really unusual. There are button-covering kits available commercially that make this so simple to do, so all you have to worry about is finding the perfect print. Here a thin hanky with a small pictorial motif has been chosen, and the covered buttons are alternated with recycled vintage clip earrings.

you will need

- thin retro-print fabric scraps
- three beaded clip-on earrings
- silver bracelet blank
- button-covering kit
- flat-nose pliers
- wire cutters
- scissors
- instant bond glue

Many an earring has been lost once removed to make a telephone call – this bracelet design makes use of all those singles.

OVER THE HUMP

1. Using the circle template provided in the button-covering kit, cut out a circle from your chosen printed fabric, making sure the part of the image you want to show is in the centre of the circle. Hold the fabric circle right-side down and centre the top half of the button on top of it. Insert the fabric with the top half of the button on top into the larger plastic cup.

2. Fold the fabric on top of the button. Push the back of the button into the plastic cup, making sure the fabric edges are tucked under it. Use the cap provided to push the button back down into the plastic cup, securing the fabric under the button back. Pop the button out of the plastic cup. Use flat-nose pliers to remove the shank from the back of the covered button.

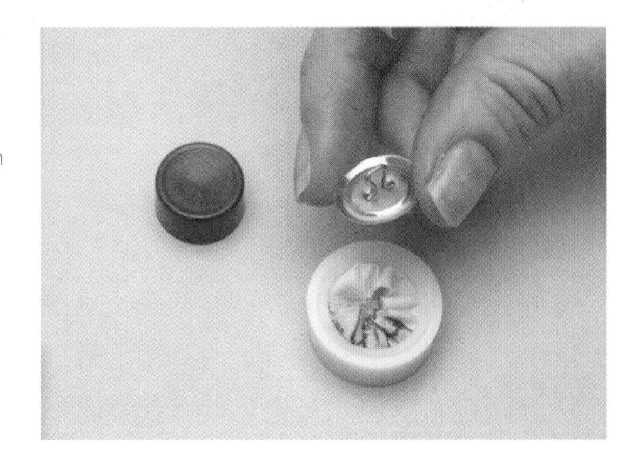

3. Use flat-nose pliers and wire cutters to remove the backs of the clip-on earrings. Apply the glue to the back of a covered button and adhere it to the first bracelet blank. Next adhere a clip-on earring. Alternate between covered buttons and beaded earrings.

gripping buttons

Use your fabric scraps to make more covered buttons and fashion yourself a stylish set of kirby grips. Look for bright and bold motifs on patterned fabric and be selective. You could make a coordinating set in different sizes.

techniques ... essential tools

2

blue lagoon necklace

It is simple to make your very own beads, so if you are feeling creative, this is the perfect project for you. Wrap the wood disks with colourful strips of fabric and fix in place with just a little glue. Different shaped wood pieces are available from craft stores, and, although a disk is nice and easy to wrap, you could try covering a heart-shaped one with red thin silk ribbon for a romantic look.

you will need

for each bead

- approx twelve 3mm x 5cm (⅛ x 2in) fabric strips
- 2cm (¾in) diameter wood disk
- paintbrush
- drill with 3mm (⅛in) drill bit
- acrylic glazing liquid
- finishing gel of your choice

for the necklace

- twenty 4mm crystal rounds
- ten Y-shaped connectors
- toggle clasp
- 0.6mm (24swg/22awg) dead soft sterling silver wire
- needle-nose pliers
- round-nose pliers
- wire cutters

1. Start by making nine fabric-wrapped beads, one at a time. Coat a disk with acrylic glazing liquid. Place the first fabric strip across the middle of the disk with the excess fabric hanging over the edges. Paint another coat of acrylic glazing liquid over the strip. Wrap the fabric tails to the back of the disk, overlapping the ends. Paint the acrylic glazing liquid over the tails. Add a second strip over the first, making a cross.

2. Add two more fabric strips, making an 'X' on top of the crossed fabric strips.

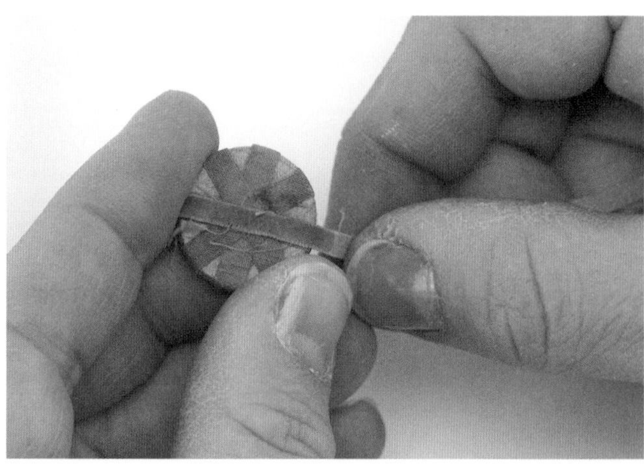

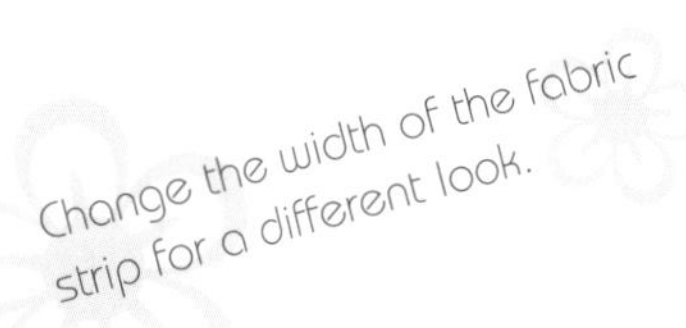

Change the width of the fabric strip for a different look.

3. Continue to add strips, filling in the gaps on the disk, always crossing the fabric strip over the centre of the disk. Once the disk is completely covered, paint another coat of acrylic glazing liquid on both sides of the disk and allow it to dry completely. Add the finishing coat of your choice and let it dry.

4. Carefully drill two holes into the bead opposite each other, and at least 3mm (⅛in) from the outer edge.

5. Cut twenty 8cm (3in) pieces of sterling silver wire. Wire wrap one piece to half of the toggle clasp (see Techniques: Making a wrapped loop). String a 4mm crystal bead onto the silver wire.

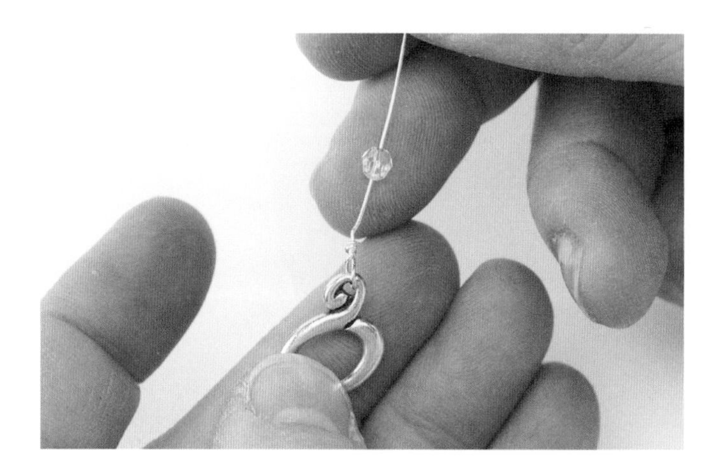

6. Wire wrap the other end of the beaded wire to one side of a Y-shaped connector.

Y-shaped connectors are sometimes hard to find. You could always try spacer beads as an alternative.

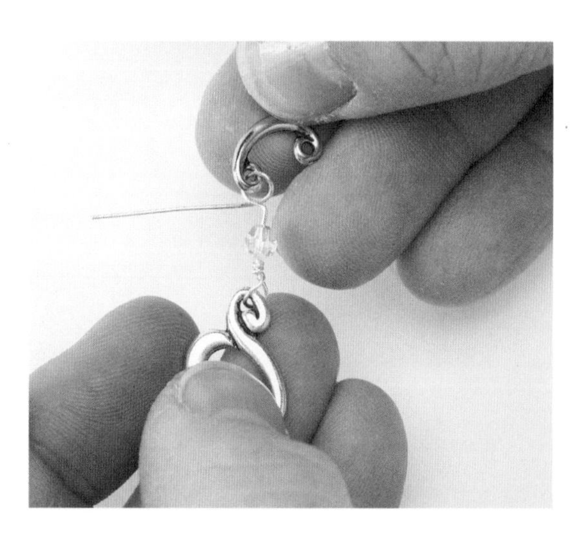

7. Wire wrap a piece of silver wire to the other side of the Y-shaped connector and string a 4mm crystal bead onto the wire. Wire wrap the other end of the wire to a fabric-wrapped bead. Continue to add to the necklace, connecting alternating Y-shaped connectors and fabric-wrapped beads with wire-wrapped crystals.

8. Wire wrap the final piece of wire to the last Y-shaped connector. Slide a 4mm bead onto the wire. Wire wrap the free end of the wire to the second half of the toggle clasp.

Make sure you keep all of the Y-shaped connectors facing in the same direction as you work.

techniques

beads

The projects in this book are made from a wide variety of beads, but these represent only a tiny proportion of the range available. There are innumerable colours, textures, shapes and sizes to suit every style of jewellery piece and each individual taste, and much of the enjoyment in making your own jewellery comes from searching for the ideal beads.

Bead shapes

Beads come in many different shapes and within each shape group there is further variety. For example, round beads are not only smooth, they can be faceted, grooved or fluted; bicones can be short or elongated; and drops can range from leaves to tear drops.

Round

Oval

Flat square

Nugget

Bicone

Rondelles

Leaf

Tear drop

Large beads

Glass beads Glass is the most versatile of all beads, available in many different shapes and sizes, from transparent to opaque, with a huge range of surface and hole-lined finishes. Pressed glass beads are made in moulds to create a range of shapes, from leaves and flowers to disks, cylinders and drops.

Crystals The term 'crystal' describes a faceted bead made from cut glass but it is often used to describe inexpensive moulded glass or even faceted plastic beads. The quantity and precision of the cutting determines the quality of sparkle and Swarovski crystals are some of the finest available on the market.

Metal beads These come in a wide range of materials, such as brass, copper, aluminium and different alloys, as well as precious metals like silver and gold. Metal beads can be moulded, modelled or shaped from sheet metal. Surface patinas can add an antique or vintage look.

Small beads

Seed beads These round, doughnut-shaped beads, also known as rocailles, range from size 3 to 15 with size 11 being the most popular. Larger seed beads are known as pebble or pony beads and the smaller ones as petites.

Triangle beads These have three sides and provide interesting texture when working bead stitches. There are two main styles, both from Japan: the geometric sharp-sided Toho triangle (see Dazzling Star Ring) and the more rounded Miyuki triangle.

Cylinder beads Also known by their trade names Delicias, Antiques or Magnificas, these precision-milled, tubular beads have a large hole which enables a thread to be passed through several times, making them ideal for bead stitching.

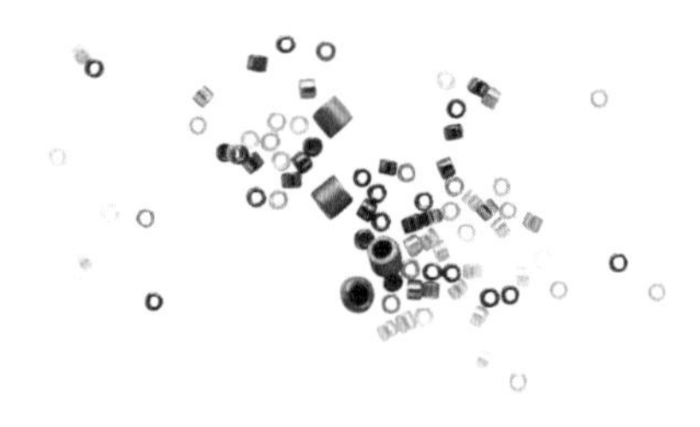

Charlottes These high-quality seed beads from the Czech Republic have a single cut facet to make them sparkle.

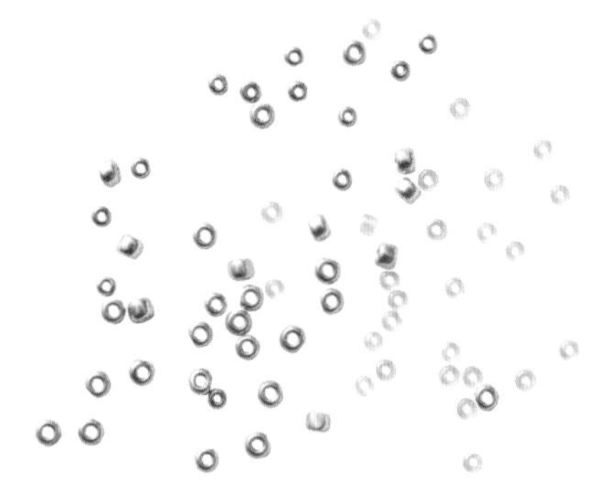

Small bead sizes Seed beads and other tiny beads are measured in either millimetres or 'aughts', written 11/100 for example, but more commonly known as size 11. The size relates to the number of seed beads that fit into 2.5cm (1in) when laid out like a row of doughnuts; the larger the number, the smaller the bead. The sizes vary between different manufacturers, but each aught size also has a corresponding size in millimetres.

Size 15	= 1.3mm
Size 11	= 1.8mm
Size 10	= 2.0mm
Size 9	= 2.2mm
Size 8	= 2.5mm
Size 6	= 3.3mm

All sorts of small elements can be incorporated into your jewellery designs from bric-a-brac to buttons, coins to charms, and even old keys.

findings & fastenings

Findings are all the little pieces, generally made of metal, that are used to make and finish items of jewellery. Fastenings are used to fasten or attach the jewellery so that it can be worn.

Eyepins Straight pieces of wire with a loop at one end; generally used to make bead links.

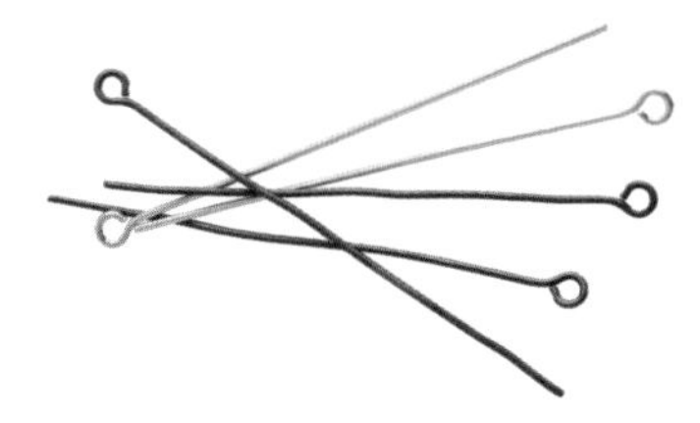

Jump rings Round or oval rings with slit for opening and closing; generally used to link components and attach fastenings.

Headpins Straight pieces of wire with flat or decorative end to stop beads falling off; used to make bead dangles.

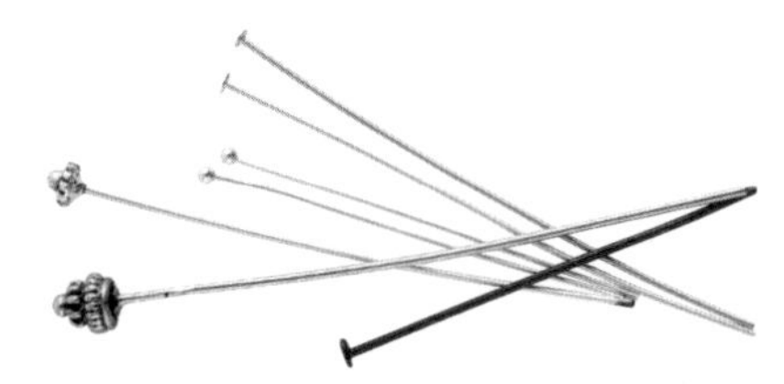

Crimp ends Specially designed for finishing bead stringing wire neatly.

Crimp beads Used to attach fastenings and space beads along beading wire; use crimping pliers or needle-nose pliers to secure in place.

Connectors Used to join elements in jewellery. They have two holes or rings and can be functional or quite decorative.

Earring wires Designed for pierced ears; shapes include kidney, fish hook, posts and hoops.

Toggle clasp Two-part fastening consisting of T-bar and hoop or ring.

Spring ring clasp Range of shapes and sizes available for fastening bracelets and necklaces.

string, wire & chain

While there are many choices of thread, wire and chain for stringing together jewellery designs, the materials described below are limited to those used for the particular projects featured in this book.

Bead stitching thread The thickness of the thread should be matched to the size of the bead holes to avoid loose beads rubbing and causing the thread to fray and snap; size D is ideal for bead stitching with seed beads. Some popular brands are Nymo™, KO™ and Superlon™.

Beading cord These unwaxed twisted threads are designed for jewellery designs where the cord is to be seen.

Hemp This traditional macramé cord is available in many different colours, including multi-coloured versions. It is available in several thicknesses, but 1mm is generally used for jewellery designs.

Chain Available in a range of metals, metallic finishes and colours, and vintage chains can also be used in your jewellery designs.

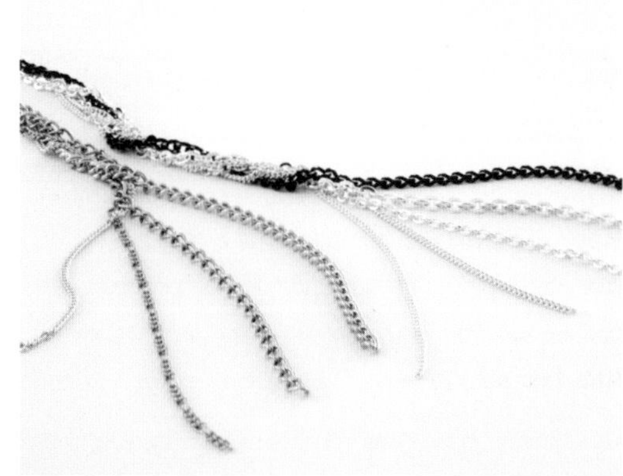

Jewellery-making wire Plated wires with a copper core are economical substitutes for sterling silver and gold, and coloured enamelled wires also make for exciting designs. Wire is available in a range of thicknesses or gauges, and it is sold in millimetres, standard wire gauge (swg) or American wire gauge (awg). The thinnest wire that will hold its shape as a bead link or plain loop is 0.6mm (24swg/22awg).

Wire is generally sold in coils and reels and as a result is curved when unwound. To take a gentle curve out of wire, fold a piece of tissue and pull the wire through between your finger and thumb, then exert pressure to straighten out the curve.

Memory wire This is an extremely hard wire that holds its circular shape, and it is available in sizes for making rings, bracelets and necklaces. It should be cut with heavyweight wire cutters.

Bead stringing wire This is composed of tiny wires or strands twisted together and coated with nylon thread. The number of strands (49, 19 or 7) determines the flexibility of the wire, and 19 strands is a good all-rounder. Match the bead hole size and weight to the diameter; 0.5mm (0.018in) is a good standard size.

essential tools

There is a wide range of tools available to help you get the best results when making jewellery. A basic tool kit of flat-nose pliers, round-nose pliers and wire cutters are beginner's requirements, but you can invest in more specialist tools as your skills develop.

Flat-nose pliers These have flat jaws with a slightly rough surface to grip wire or findings. Some are called snipe- or chain-nose pliers, which taper towards the tip, and others have a blunt end (blunt-nose pliers).
Round-nose pliers These have tubular tapered jaws and are used for coiling, bending wire and making jump rings. Work near the tip of the jaws for tiny loops, but towards the base for larger rings.
Wire cutters Known as side or end cutters depending on the position of the cutting jaws, these are essential for cutting and trimming wire.
Crimp pliers Used to secure crimp ends and crimp beads for a more professional finish.

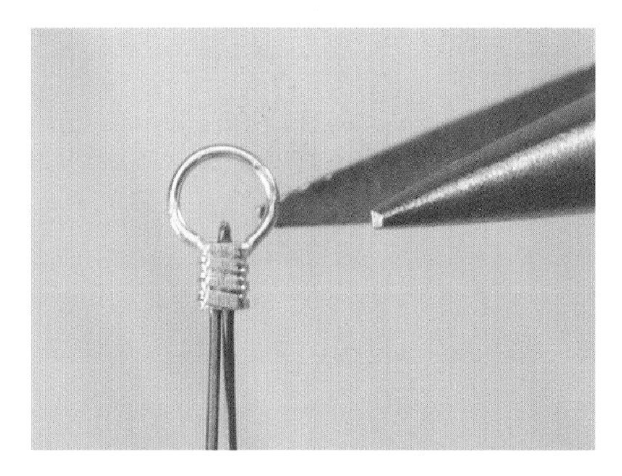

Flat-nose pliers

Wire cutters

Round-nose pliers

Crimp pliers

essential glues

There are several types of glue used for jewellery making. Always work in a well-ventilated area and take particular care when using instant bond glue as it sticks to skin. A cocktail stick (toothpick) is useful for applying tiny amounts of glue.

Epoxy resin A very strong, two-part glue used to secure metal and heavy embellishments, such as stones, glass and beads. Look for quick setting glue that dries clear.

Jewellery glue Clear glue that takes a little while to dry but remains flexible when it sets. It is generally used for securing knots and popular makes include E6000 and G-S Hypo Cement.

Instant bond Also called superglue, this sets very quickly but dries hard and may become brittle and break.

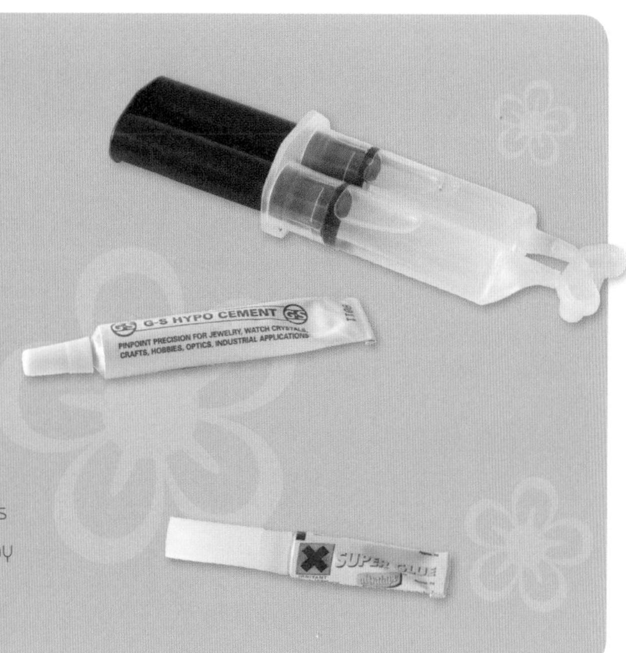

making a felt ball bead

Wet felting using wool fibres is an easy way to make large, lightweight beads, and these can be embellished further, with seed beads for example. A hard bead will hold its shape well when cut in half.

1. Pull out a small bit of wool roving. Wind up into a ball, keeping the fine wool fibres at the end wrapped around the ball. The ball will shrink to about half its size as it felts, so start with a bigger ball than the size of bead you want.

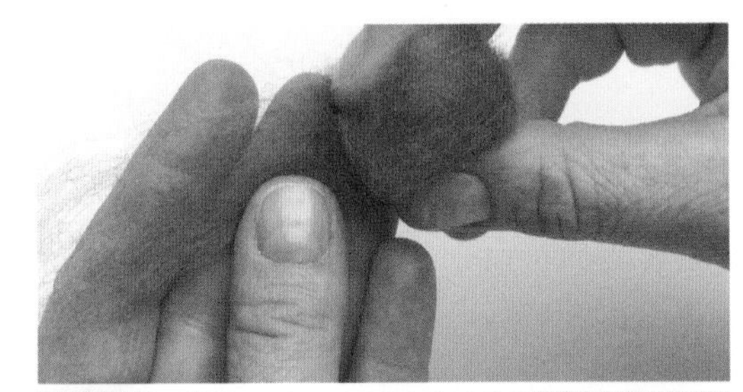

2. Fill a basin with warm water and a little soap to help the wool fibres open, and submerge the ball. Add a tiny drop of soap to your hands and begin gently rolling the ball. Gentle pressure in the beginning will ensure the bead is round and smooth without any folds over the surface. Dip the felt back in the warm water every three or four rolls. Continue rolling until the ball starts to condense a bit.

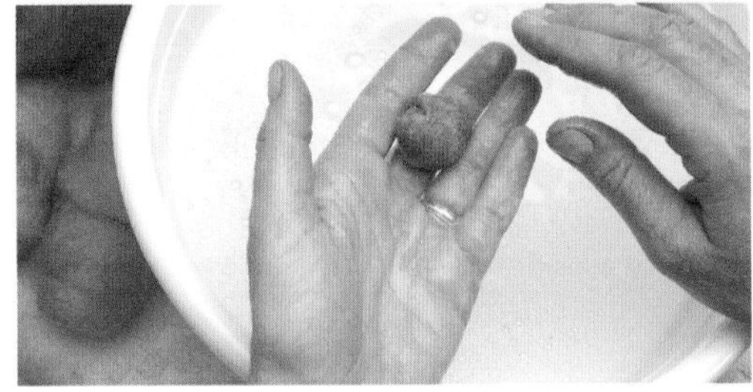

3. Add more soap to your hands and begin adding a bit more pressure as you roll, continuing to dip the ball in the sudsy water every so often. The bead is ready when it feels very firm and compact when you squish it; once it is the correct size, rinse in clear water and blot dry by rolling on a towel.

wirework techniques

Wire is a versatile material that allows a great degree of freedom to form shapes and create structure in your designs. Wirework is the term used to describe making wire jewellery and components, and the key techniques used to make the projects featured in this book are explained here.

Opening and closing a jump ring

Never open a jump ring by pulling the ends outward as this will weaken and distort the shape of the component. Ideally work with two flat-nose or chain-nose pliers.

1. Begin by grasping the jump ring on both sides with two pairs of flat-nose pliers. Open the jump ring laterally, moving one end toward you and one end away from you.

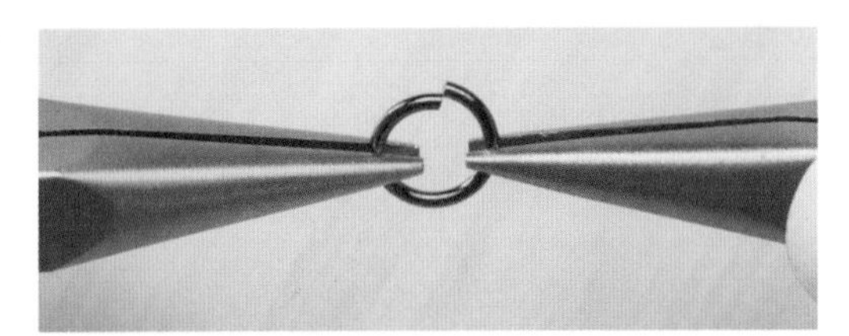

2. To close the ring, grasp it again on both sides with the pliers. Gently compress the ends together as you bring them past one another. Continue gently compressing them as you bring them back together. When they come together the second time, you should hear and feel a click. This indicates that the ring is closed with tension and will remain closed until you open it again. If it doesn't click, brush the ends past one another again until you secure them with tension.

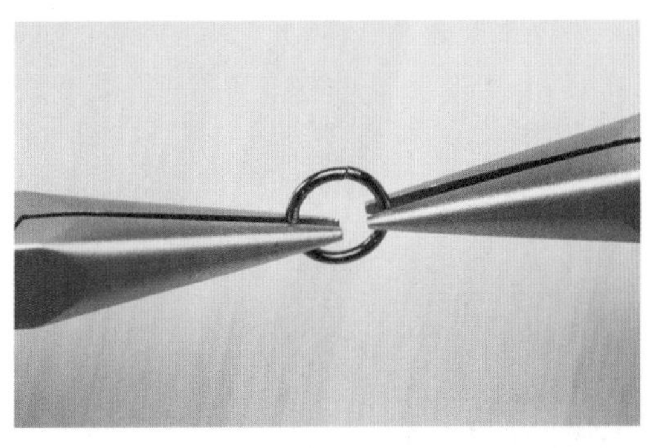

To open and close an earring wire loop, place one set of pliers on the coiled section and the other next to the loop opening.

Making bead links and dangles

Resembling large dressmaker's pins, headpins are used to make bead dangles or charms, which can then be hung from chain for bracelets and necklaces, or attached to earring wires. Eyepins are similar but have a large loop at one end for making bead links.

Making a plain loop

1. Pick up the beads required using a headpin for a dangle and an eyepin for a link. Trim the wire to 7mm–1cm (⅜–½in). The distance will depend on the thickness of the wire and the size of the loop required. Make a right-angled bend close to the top bead using snipe-nose pliers.

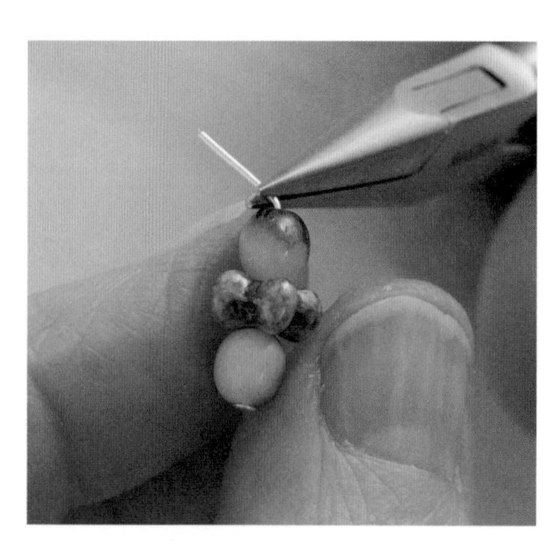

2. Hold the tip of the wire with round-nosed pliers and rotate the pliers to bend the wire partway around the tip. The distance you hold the wire down from the top of the pliers will determine the size of the loop.

3. Reposition the pliers by flipping your wrist, then continue to rotate the wire around until the tip touches the wire again to produce a loop in the middle.

Making a wrapped loop

This is stronger than the plain loop and ideal for beads with slightly larger holes. The method describes working a wrapped loop on a headpin to create a dangle; to make a bead link you will need to work with cut pieces of wire, creating a wrapped wire loop at either end, as you join it to another bead link, to a connector or to a clasp.

1. Use longer headpins to allow for the wrapping – you will need at least 3cm (1¼in) of wire above the last bead. Pick up the beads required and, using snipe-nose pliers, hold the wire above the top bead, leaving a small gap; bend at a right-angle.

2. Hold the wire close to the bend with round-nose pliers and wrap the tail all the way round to form a loop. Bring the wire right round so that it is at right-angles to the wire inside the beads.

3. Hold the loop flat in snipe-nose pliers and wind the wire tail around the stem covering the gap between the loop and the bead. If you find it difficult to wrap the wire by hand, use flat-nose pliers for more purchase. Trim the tail.

beading techniques

Bead stitches can be worked with needle and thread to make beaded fabric with a quite sculptural effect. The important thing is to use even-sized beads.

Making a plain bezel

A bezel, worked in circular peyote stitch, is a rim of tiny seed beads that goes just over the edge of a large stone or cabochon. By using progressively smaller beads, the beadwork curves in to enclose the cabochon and grip it securely.

1. String an even number of beads (for example, size 11 hexagonal beads) to surround the cabochon, tie in a circle and pass the needle through a few beads to hide the knot, leaving a long tail. These beads form the first two rounds of circular peyote stitch.

2. Pick up a bead on the needle, miss a bead on the circle and pass the needle through the next bead along. Continue adding beads one at a time by missing a bead and passing the needle through the next bead along.

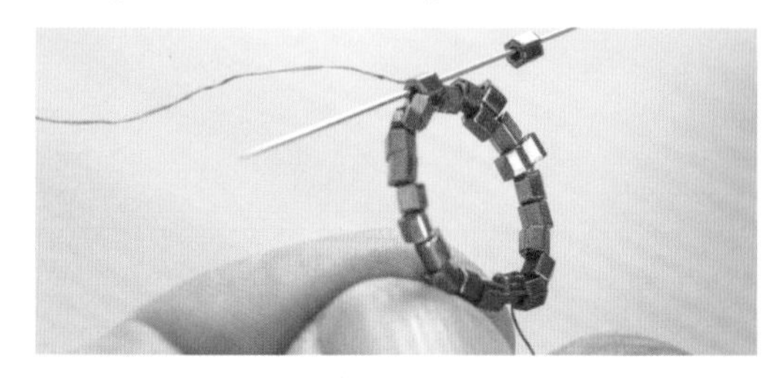

3. At the end of the round take the needle through the first bead added to 'step up' ready to begin the next round. The beadwork has a distinctive zigzag edge with 'up' and 'down' beads.

4. Change to size 11 seed beads and continue adding between the 'up' beads from the previous round. Remember to step up through the first bead added in each subsequent round.

5. Add a round of size 15 cylinder beads and pull up tight, then a final round with tiny beads (size 15 charlottes) to make a smooth thin edge on the collar. Take the thread through to the beginning row again.

6. Insert the cabochon face down and repeat the peyote stitch from step 4 to create a second beaded collar that holds the cabochon securely, again finishing with tiny charlottes.

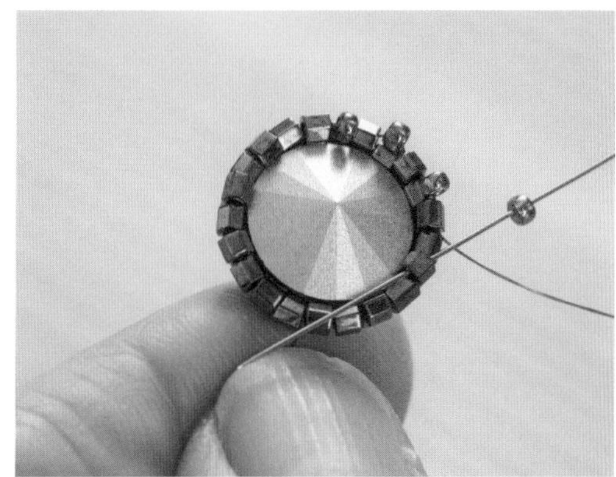

Making a frilled collar bezel

Use circular herringbone stitch to add a flat collar to the bezel; to force the collar to flare out and wave impressively, use peyote stitch between the herringbone stacks.

1. Bring the beading thread out between two beads in the middle of the three rows of cylinder beads on the edge of the bezel. Pick up two size 11 seed beads and go through the next hexagon along. Continue all the way round.

2. Step up through the first seed bead again. On the next round work a herringbone stitch on each pair of beads, adding a floating bead between each stack.

3. Finish the first round of herringbone stitch with a single floating bead between each stack. Step up at the end of the round.

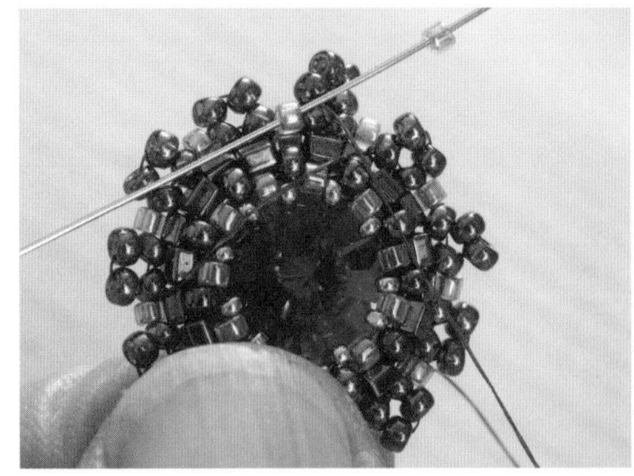

4. On the next round, step up and add the first two beads as herringbone stitch, then work peyote stitch: pick up a seed bead and go through the floating bead. Pick up another seed bead and go through the first seed bead in the next stack ready to work another herringbone stitch.

5. Continue all the way round, alternating between herringbone and peyote stitch. On the next round you will work peyote stitch again between the stacks, adding three beads this time. Each subsequent round has more seed beads in the peyote stitch section causing it to wave dramatically.

Fancy stones with foil backing have a wonderful depth to their sparkle and when surrounded by a beaded bezel this effect is enhanced, and it is like looking into a deep pool. Bezels can be left plain to create a simple ring or you can add a decorative collar.

beader's knots

There are several simple knots that you will need to be able to tie when jewellery making, to ensure your pieces remain intact and fastenings firmly attached. For extra security, add a drop of jewellery glue on the knots and leave to dry before trimming the tails.

Half-hitch knot

Take the needle behind a thread between beads and pull through leaving a loop. Pass the needle back through the loop and pull up to make the half-hitch. Work a second half-hitch a few beads along for extra security, applying a drop of jewellery glue before trimming the tail.

A useful addition to your tool kit is a pair of fine pointed tweezers, which can come in very useful when you need to untie a knot.

Reef (square) knot

Pass the left thread over the right and tuck under. Then pass the right thread over the left and tuck under the left thread and through the gap in the middle of the knot.

Overhand knot

Cross the tail over the main thread to make a small loop, then pass the tail under the thread and back through the loop. Pull on each end of the thread to tighten the knot. You can manoeuvre the knot into position with a tapestry needle.

Tying an overhand knot with a loop

This is a useful variation of the overhand knot. Instead of pulling the entire length of the strand through the knot, pull out a folded end to form a tight loop. The loop often functions as part of the clasp (see Love Macramé Bracelet).

1. Fold the cord end down against itself. The length will depend on the size of the loop you want to make.

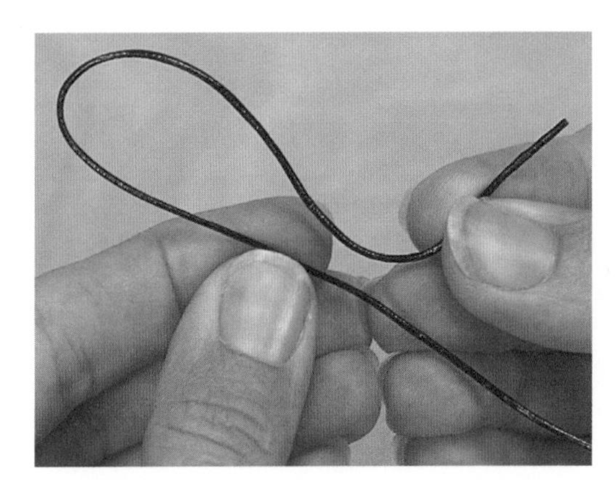

2. Wrap both cord thicknesses into a circle loop under the fold.

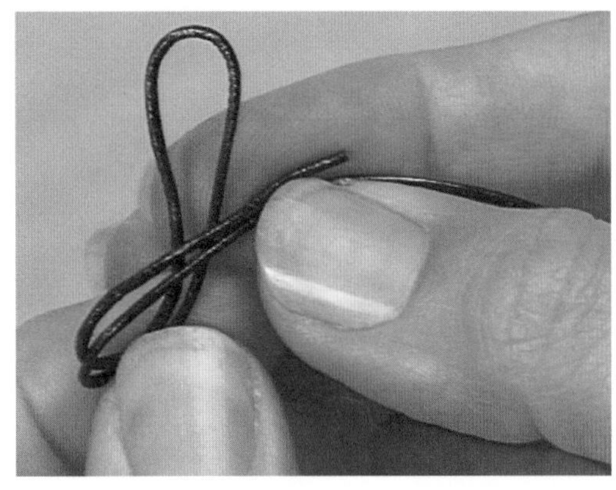

3. Bring the fold around and through the loop, then pull to tighten. If necessary, trim the cord end where it comes out from under the finished knot.

designer credits

The publishers would like to thank the following designers who have allowed the reproduction of their designs in this book.

Heidi Boyd

Beaded Leaf Bracelet

Gemstone Wired Cuff

Ocean Swirl Ring

Love Macramé Bracelet

Julie Collings

Sparkly Flower Ring

Becky Meverden

Korean Maedeup Earrings

Jennifer Perkins

Cute Retro Bracelet

Margot Potter

Bird's Nest Earrings

Bright Button Necklace

Heidi Pridemore

Polka-Dot Necklace

Twilight Necklace

Blue Lagoon Necklace

Susan Ray

Ivory Rose Cuff

Shirley Rufener

Asian-Inspired Earrings

Strawberry-Thief Bracelet

Dorothy Wood

Classic Bronze Chain

Dazzling Star Ring

Jean Yates

Charming Teacup Bracelet

index

A DAVID & CHARLES BOOK

David & Charles is an imprint of
F&W Media International, Ltd
Brunel House, Forde Close,
Newton Abbot, TQ12 4PU, UK

F&W Media International, Ltd is a subsidiary of
F+W Media, Inc
10151 Carver Road, Suite #200,
Blue Ash, OH 45242, USA

First published in the UK and USA in 2012

A catalogue record for this book is
available from the British Library.

ISBN-13: 978-1-4463-0241-5 hardback
ISBN-10: 1-4463-0241-5 hardback

Printed in China by RR Donnelley for:
F&W Media International, Ltd
Brunel House, Forde Close,
Newton Abbot, TQ12 4PU, UK

10 9 8 7 6 5 4 3 2 1

Acquisitions Editor: Jeni Hennah

Assistant Editor: Grace Harvey

Project Editor: Cheryl Brown

Designer: Lisa Fordham

Photographers: Alias Imaging, LLC, Karl Adamson,
Hal Barkin, John Carrico, Ric Deliantoni, Tim
Grondin, Adam Henry, Adam Leigh-Manuell,
Becky Meverden, Curt Meverden, Al Parrish,
Christine Polomsky, Shirley Rufener, Kim Sayer,
Ally Stuart, Simon Whitmore, Lorna Yabsley

Production Controller: Kelly Smith

loved this book?

For more inspiration, ideas and free downloadable projects visit:

www.stitchcraftcreate.com

Bake Me I'm Yours... Just for Fun

Various

ISBN-13: 978-1-4463-0069-5

Be inspired to get crafty with this diverse collection of 20 fabulous projects. Create unique gifts and accessories, and discover a range of craft techniques such as sewing, knitting, papercraft and felting.

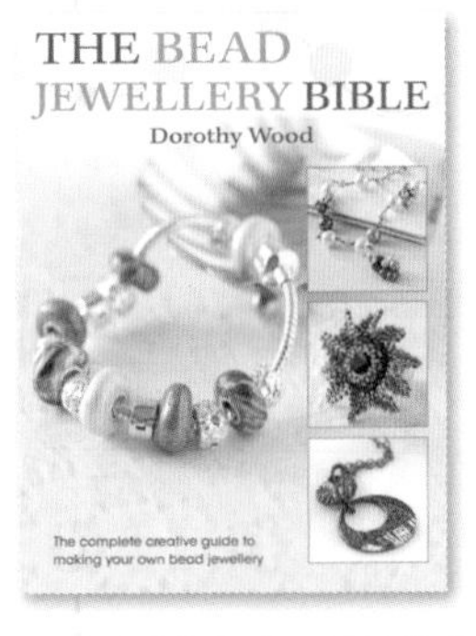

The Bead Jewellery Bible

Dorothy Wood

ISBN-13: 978-0-7153-3870-4

Create unique bead jewellery with a truly professional finish. With 12 step-by-step projects to get you started and all the techniques and ideas needed to create your own, this is the ultimate resource for making bead jewellery!

Simply Beaded Bliss

Heidi Boyd

ISBN-13: 978-1-6006-1095-0

Get ready to break tradition and combine beads with common materials used in unconventional ways to make beautiful jewellery. Learn how to use nail polish to create the look of enamel and link together cut up credit cards into a bracelet!

The Impatient Beader Gets Inspired

Margot Potter

ISBN-13: 978-1-5818-0854-4

Find your inner art girl! Inspiration is all around you, and this book whelps you make the most of it. You'll discover a delightful diversity of techniques like decoupage, soldering, embroidery, Hot Fix crystal application, polymer clay and more.

All details correct at time of printing.

ALPH